The Guatemalan Tax Reform

The Guatemalan
Tax Reform

Roy Bahl,
Jorge Martinez-Vazquez,
and Sally Wallace

WestviewPress
A Division of HarperCollins*Publishers*

336.205
B15g

Copyright © 1996 by Westview Press, A Division of HarperCollins Publishers, Inc.

Published in 1996 in the United States of America by Westview Press, 5500 Central Avenue, Boulder, Colorado 80301-2877, and in the United Kingdom by Westview Press, 12 Hid's Copse Road, Cumnor Hill, Oxford OX2 9JJ

Library of Congress Cataloging-in-Publication Data
Bahl, Roy W.
   The Guatemalan tax reform / by Roy Bahl, Jorge Martinez-Vazquez, and Sally Wallace.
      p. cm.
   Includes bibliographical references.
   ISBN 0-8133-8928-3
   1. Taxation—Guatemala.   I. Martinez-Vazquez, Jorge.
II. Wallace, Sally.   III. Title.
HJ2474.B34   1996
336.2'05'097281—dc20   96-9319
                                                                              CIP

The paper used in this publication meets the requirements of the American National Standard for Permanence of Paper for Printed Library Materials Z39.48-1984.

10   9   8   7   6   5   4   3   2   1

Contents

Preface

This book describes the analysis that led to the reform of the Guatemalan tax system in 1992. The Guatemala Fiscal Administration Project was initiated in 1989 with the objective of assisting the government in a revision of the tax system to make it more fair and more conducive to economic growth. The work began at a time when the Guatemalan economy was reeling: high inflation, low growth, and a fiscal deficit. The Project lived through two presidents and five ministers of finance.

The overall scope of work was broader than the tax policy aspects described here and included major efforts to improve tax administration, budgeting and fiscal planning, and a training program in customs and tax administration. The results of these activities are described in a comprehensive final report prepared by the Policy Economics Group of KPMG Peat Marwick.

The policy work was successful in that a comprehensive tax reform passed the Guatemalan congress in 1992. It broadened the base of the income and value-added taxes and increased the revenue share of GDP. It significantly improved the horizontal equity of the tax system; it did not harm the vertical equity; it eliminated some harmful economic distortions; and it simplified the tax structure, thereby facilitating administration and compliance. Professors Roy Bahl and Jorge Martinez-Vazquez served as the Project directors for the tax policy reform.

This book is authored by Professors Bahl, Martinez-Vazquez, and Wallace but is based on the work of all of those who were involved in the Guatemala tax reform studies. KPMG did most of the revenue estimation that is underneath the tables presented here and in many cases prepared the basic tables. Background papers on tax policy analysis were carried out by a number of authors, as is noted in the references and the list of technical papers at the back of this book. Some of the best public finance economists in the world were involved in the background work for this book. We draw extensively on their technical papers. Arthur Turner and Peggy Stanley did an excellent job of preparing this manuscript for publication.

The Project began under the direction of Minister Rodolfo Paez, who played an important part in the design of the Project. It ended under the direction of Minister Richard Aitkenhead. Minister Aitkenhead led the design of the reform program and the selling of its components to the Guatemalan congress and the public.

The Guatemala Fiscal Administration Project was carried out under a contract with the U.S. Agency for International Development (Contract No. 520-0371-C-00-1093). KPMG was the prime contractor with responsibility for tax administration, development of the models, and overall coordination. Georgia State University was responsible for organizing and carrying out the tax policy analysis that is reported in this book.

Roy Bahl
Jorge Martinez-Vazquez
Sally Wallace

The Guatemalan Tax Reform

1

The Macroeconomic Setting
for Tax Reform

Guatemala's 1992 tax reform was prompted by an economic crisis. Throughout the decade of the 1980s, the macroeconomic situation was one of relative disequilibrium and instability, with low rates of real economic growth, rates of inflation that were very high by Guatemalan standards, devaluation of the quetzal (Q), chronic deficits in the balance of payments (and hence dwindling international reserves), and continually growing difficulties in servicing external debt. The situation deteriorated markedly between 1990 and 1992, and fiscal imbalance became a severe problem.

The fiscal deficit exceeded 2.5 percent of gross domestic product (GDP) in 1990, and real tax collections were lower in 1991 than in 1988 by 1.3 percent of GDP. Real per capita government spending levels were falling in the early 1990s, and potential sources of foreign borrowing had all but been exhausted. During 1991, the government attempted to shore up its fiscal position with a number of temporary measures: a tax amnesty, a one-time charge on gross income of companies, and a surcharge on petroleum products. Current expenditures were also reduced significantly. These temporary measures did succeed in reducing the fiscal deficit significantly, to 0.4 percent of GDP in 1991, but did not address the underlying problems. It was evident that the Guatemalan government would have to enact a fiscal program in 1992.

Authors' Note: This description of the macroeconomy in Guatemala is based on our field work, Government of Guatemala Reports and Analyses, analyses of the IMF "Recent Economic Developments" reports, the World Bank Country Economic Memorandums, and the economic reports of the Inter-American Development Bank (IDB, 1991, 1992).

Raising additional revenues to deal with a budget deficit was only one of the three major issues that would have to be addressed by such a program. The others were a flawed tax structure and an inadequate tax administration. The results of these structural and administrative shortcomings were a slow growth in government revenues; unfairness in the distribution of tax burdens among families at different income levels, among similarly situated families, and among businesses; and interference with economic choices. It was recognized that the solution to Guatemala's short-term fiscal crisis would have to include a tax increase, but it was also recognized that in the longer run, the more chronic problems could not be resolved without a comprehensive reform of the tax structure and the tax administration.

The Economy in the Pre-1986 Period

From a historical perspective, Guatemala's economy performed satisfactorily prior to 1980. Traditional exports (coffee, cotton, bananas, and sugar) and industrial production fueled by a policy of import substitution within the Central American Common Market (CACM) were the main engines of growth in the 1960-1979 period when GDP grew at an average rate of 5.5 percent. Prior to the first oil shock in 1973, Guatemala enjoyed a particularly stable price level, with an average inflation rate of 1.5 percent between 1946 and 1972. Between 1973 and 1979 the average inflation rate of 12 percent never reached the extremely high levels of other Latin American countries. However, most observers see the 1970s as the period when Guatemala developed most of the problems it faced in the next decade. High rates of effective protection with respect to trade outside the CACM, an overvalued exchange rate after 1972, and preferential credit policies for domestic businesses (which typically were able to borrow at negative real interest rates), were all responsible for an industrial sector that, despite very low labor costs, was not internationally competitive and absorbed little labor input.

In 1980, Guatemala entered a deep recession that lasted for more than five years. By the end of 1985 GDP per capita had fallen to levels of the late 1960s. The depth of the recession was due to a combination of domestic and international factors. Political instability in the region kept away foreign investors. Internal unrest and a severely overvalued exchange rate also led to capital flight. The international recession of the early 1980s and large reductions in the prices of traditional exports led to higher interest rates for international loans and to a deterioration in the terms of trade. But perhaps the most important factor in the depth of the recession was the collapse of the CACM. Economic policies during this period were characterized by growing fiscal deficits, frequently financed by increases in the money supply and, toward the end of the period, by the introduction of multiple exchange rates.

In 1983, the military regime attempted a stabilization plan with International Monetary Fund (IMF) assistance. The plan called for a reduction in public expenditures and a tax reform. The latter was ambitious in scope: a new value-added tax (VAT) was introduced with a 10 percent rate, the income tax was modified, the stamp tax was eliminated, and export taxes were reduced. The 1983 Guatemala tax reform was preceded by little preparation for the administration of the new VAT. Perhaps also because of little preparation, the reform was characterized by indecision. The VAT rate was reduced from 10 percent to 7 percent only a few months after the introduction of the tax, and the stamp taxes were brought back in 1984. An attempt by the military regime to introduce new fiscal measures in April 1985 faced strong opposition from the private sector and did not succeed.

The Cerezo Administration

The Cerezo administration began with positive economic growth in 1986. The average growth rate in real GDP during the 1986-1990 period was 3.6 percent. But the economy tended to deteriorate, and fundamental imbalances in the central government and international accounts became prominent during the last year of the Cerezo administration. By the end of 1990, it appeared that this administration would leave the economy in no better shape than it had found it in 1986.

To be sure, the fundamental imbalances did not develop overnight. In the external sector, imports grew at a brisk pace after early 1987, fueled by continuous growth in private and public spending. However, exports grew at a more moderate pace because of sluggish nontraditional exports and a deterioration in the terms of trade for traditional exports over most of the period. Net capital inflows declined after a high in 1987, led by a marked drop in private capital net inflows. Despite repeated devaluations of the quetzal and a floating exchange rate beginning in 1990, Guatemala's net reserve position faced increased pressure over the period. By the end of 1990, the government had defaulted on most of its international loans, including those from the World Bank and the International Monetary Fund.

Guatemala's central government economic policies experienced a continuous deterioration after the first year of Cerezo's administration. By most accounts, fiscal policy was the main problem. The administration inherited public finances in disarray and left the same legacy to its successors.

The package of fiscal measures introduced in 1986 was intended, for the short run, to close the fiscal gap. These measures included an extraordinary tax on exports (to be phased out gradually), a temporary tax on international phone calls, and a selective consumption tax. The most important fiscal move of the Cerezo administration was the tax reform of 1987. This reform was the fundamental piece of the *Programa de Reordenamiento Economica y Social* (a collection of policies initially agreed to by the private sector) that was oriented to promote a strategy of economic growth led by private exports. By 1987, the administration also began to put more emphasis on the need to undertake an ambitious domestic investment program in social sector areas (mainly education and health) to pay for what was termed the "social debt." The private sector saw this program as creating more bureaucracy and exacerbating the government deficit and, to some extent, used it to oppose the tax reform.

The tax reform succeeded at first in increasing the central government's share of GDP from 8.8 percent in 1986 to 11.1 percent in 1988 (Table 1.1). This exceeded the revenue target for the reform. Actually, when non-tax revenues are excluded, the share of tax revenue collections in GDP went from 6.9 percent in 1986 to 8.8 percent in 1988. However, the share of government revenues in GDP fell back to 10.1 percent in 1989 and plunged to 8.1 percent in 1990. If we consider only tax revenues, the shares were 7.9 percent and 6.9 percent, for 1989 and 1990 respectively. There is still disagreement over what was behind this dismal performance, but most fingers pointed to a dramatic decrease in compliance, perhaps as high as 25 percent in 1990. If this is an accurate estimate of the deterioration of the compliance rate, the tax system still should have yielded revenues over one-quarter higher than what was actually produced. In 1989, while GDP increased by 15.5 percent in nominal terms, central government revenues were up only 4 percent.

In contrast, government expenditures grew from a 10.8 percent share of GDP in 1986 to 13.0 percent in 1988, before dropping to 10.6 percent in 1990. The central government deficit reached Q800 million, or 2.5 percent of GDP, in 1990. The projected deficit for the central government in 1991 was revised early in the year to about Q2 billion.[1]

An important source of the consolidated deficits in the public sector had been the so-called quasi-fiscal deficit. These were mainly losses of the Bank of Guatemala that arose from subsidies for protected exchange rates and subsidized interest rates. The quasi-fiscal deficit alone represented 1.8 percent of GDP in 1989. The rest of the nonfinancial public sector—social security system, public enterprises, local government, and the universities—traditionally has operated with a surplus. Of these institutions,

TABLE 1.1 Revenue Collections as a Percent of GDP

	1984	1985	1986	1987	1988	1989	1990	1991	1992
Total Current Revenues[a]	6.93	7.63	8.80	10.38	11.07	10.08	8.12	9.75	10.63
Less: Non-tax Revenues	1.62	1.94	1.87	2.20	2.26	2.22	1.19	2.52	2.37
Equals: Tax Revenues	5.31	5.69	6.94	8.18	8.80	7.86	6.93	7.23	8.25
Income Taxes	0.83	0.97	1.07	1.42	2.01	1.72	1.49	2.10	1.78
Individuals	0.31	0.32	0.32	0.40	0.46	0.30	0.26	0.36	0.33
Businesses	0.52	0.65	0.75	1.02	1.56	1.41	1.23	1.74	1.45
Value-Added Tax	1.51	1.92	1.95	2.32	2.41	2.35	2.33	2.20	2.64
Customs Duties	0.84	0.71	0.86	1.54	1.89	1.71	1.54	1.40	2.13
Excise Taxes	1.18	1.12	0.93	1.17	1.08	0.93	1.20	1.24	1.38
Export Taxes	0.30	0.09	1.34	0.85	0.50	0.23	0.01	0.00	0.00
All Other	0.66	0.89	0.78	0.87	0.91	0.92	0.37	0.29	0.32

[a]Detail may not correspond to totals because of rounding.
Source: Ministry of Finance, Government of Guatemala, as reported to *Consultoria Para La Administracion Fiscal*, Policy Economics Group, KPMG Peat Marwick, and Policy Research Program, Georgia State University, 1991-1993.

however, only the Social Security Institute (IGSS) operated with a true surplus, averaging 0.5 percent of GDP from 1986 to 1990. Local governments and universities showed a surplus position during this period because of the central government revenue-sharing provisions incorporated in Guatemala's constitution. As for the two larger public enterprises, the phone company (GUATEL) was profitable, but its surplus remained negligible because of large capital spending programs, and the electric company (INDE) received quite large foreign exchange subsidies from the Bank of Guatemala.

The financing requirements of the public sector were partially offset in the first few years of the Cerezo administration by foreign aid, mainly budgetary support from USAID. As the government deficit loomed larger in the last year of the administration, foreign aid was significantly reduced, and the government resorted to an expansion of domestic credit. The monetization of the deficit led to an acceleration of the inflation rate, and by the end of 1990, the inflation rate had reached 60 percent. There was an attempt by the Cerezo administration to introduce new tax legislation in the summer of 1990 with the hope of increasing (or at least containing the decline of) tax revenues. The measures included the elimination of a number of incentive laws, new taxes on foreign exchange operations, increases in a number of fees, and the introduction of a tax amnesty. Only a few of the measures were eventually approved in Congress, and it was too little, too late to make any noticeable difference.

The Serrano Administration

The government of Jorge Serrano took office in January 1991 and confronted the need to implement a short-run stabilization plan to deal with the fiscal deficit, and a long-term economic plan. Without a World Bank/IMF-sanctioned stabilization plan, the options for the new government were few: the availability of foreign loans was practically nil, foreign grants had dried up, and the ability to borrow from the public and the private banking system was limited.

The general economic conditions faced by the Serrano administration were similar to those faced by the Cerezo administration early in 1986. Fiscal imbalance remained the core problem. But there were also problems with the management of the exchange rate and negative real rates of interest in the financial sector that aggravated the significance of capital flight. Both the Cerezo administration and the previous military regimes had introduced major tax reforms (1983 and 1987), and both administrations also attempted minor changes in the tax system before and after the major reforms, always under pressure to increase tax collections.

The Serrano administration's approach to the plethora of problems it inherited was to initiate a stabilization plan designed specifically to regain balance in the fiscal and external sectors. The stabilization plan, decreasing the fiscal deficit and tightening the money supply, met with initial success in 1991. The fiscal measures to implement this program included a temporary, compulsory allocation of bonds among businesses and higher income individuals, some minor tax measures, significant cuts in public expenditures, and the transfer of increased profits from state enterprises, resulting from lower international oil prices. Monetary policy measures included an intensification of open market operations and an increase in the reserve requirements for the banking system.

The central government account actually recorded a small surplus in 1991, and the overall public sector deficit, including the quasi-fiscal transfers and losses of the Bank of Guatemala, was down to 1.2 percent of GDP for 1991. This turnaround in policy was accompanied by a moderation in the annual inflation rate to 10 percent and a rate of growth in real GDP of 3.3 percent over 1991. The tight monetary policy stance during 1991 led also to positive real rates of interest and a return of capital which in past years had fled abroad (IDB 1992, pp. 98-104).

Total revenue collections as a percent of GDP rebounded in 1991 to 9.8 percent from 8.1 percent in 1990 (Table 1.1). Most of this overall revenue improvement was the result of temporary measures such as the one time compulsory allocation of government bonds. The increase in tax revenues was much less significant: 7.2 percent of GDP in 1991 as compared with 6.9 percent in 1990.

The government fiscal program for 1992, approved in July, included a comprehensive tax reform package, accompanied by an extensive tax administration modernization effort. The program had the objectives of increasing the overall efficiency of the tax system and raising total government revenues to 9.8 percent of GDP in 1993. This target was surpassed by the end of 1992, with actual total revenues representing 10.6 percent of GDP. The tax reform program, which is discussed extensively throughout this report, included the widening of the tax base for the VAT and the income tax; a simplification of several taxes, including the personal and company income taxes; the inclusion of some stamp taxes in the VAT; and increase in excises, in particular those on petroleum products. The reform succeeded in increasing the tax revenue share of GDP—it was up by one percent in 1992—but this is less than had been originally planned.

The tax reform was accompanied in October by the liberalization of the foreign trade regime, which lowered the top tariff rates and narrowed most tariff rates to the 20 percent to 5 percent range, eliminated the 3 percent import surcharge, and eliminated many custom tariff exemptions.

The tax reform was also accompanied by a comprehensive reform of the tax administration apparatus. The Supreme Court created a special court to accelerate review and sentencing in tax evasion cases. An integral tax audit program was initiated also in 1993 using third-party information to prosecute evasion in sectors of the economy that were notorious in the past for lack of compliance. The taxpayer identification numbering system, which had been in development over a long period of time, was finally completed. Computerized information services were also enhanced in several areas of customs, such as the Vehicle Appraisal Program that reduced the discretion of Customs' personnel in the classification and valuation of imported vehicles. A system of personnel rotation was introduced in Customs' posts, and minimum collection targets were established for each post.

These significant reforms in 1992 were complemented with additional measures in policy and tax administration during 1993. Congress has continued the discussion of a simplified property (land) tax in substitution of the self-assessed property tax that had been hastily introduced in 1991. The proposed new land tax would increase government revenues by about 0.2 percent of GDP. In addition, the 1993 Congress approved a number of changes to the *Código Tributario*, significantly stiffening the penalties for tax evasion. Meanwhile, the number of tax auditors was doubled, and training, manuals, and practices were significantly improved.

The accomplishments on the revenue side of the budget were complemented in 1992 and 1993 by an austere public expenditure policy. With the exception of an overdue increase in the wages and salaries of public employees in 1992, other public expenditures were cut or frozen. For example, the government issued a freeze on all unspent allocations by the middle of 1992 and a one-third across-the-board cut in all budget appropriations for the rest of the year. The 1993 budget allowed for new hirings only in education and health and increased expenditures only for capital investments.

The relatively good performance of the economy was sustained through 1992, with an average inflation rate around 14 percent, positive real rates of interest, a consolidated deficit of the entire public sector in the neighborhood of 1 percent of GDP, a rate of growth in real GDP of over 4.5 percent, and an increase in international reserves. During 1993, the challenge continued to be the containment of the consolidated deficit of the public sector, the maintenance of a conservative monetary policy to keep the liquidity of financial markets under control with positive real rates of interest, and the allowance of a moderate devaluation of the quetzal to reflect the decrease in the terms of trade. Another important element of economic policy for 1993 was the gradual deregulation of oil prices. The inflation rate in Guatemala is not low by international standards.[2]

Notes

1. IMF (1993) reports the following exchange rates, in quetzales per U.S. dollar. These were used throughout the study:

1980	1.000
1985	1.000
1986	1.875
1987	2.500
1988	2.620
1989	2.816
1990	4.486
1991	5.029
1992	5.170
1993	5.635

2. The increase in consumer prices in Guatemala was about average by comparison with other Latin American countries in 1992 but was substantially higher in 1991.

2

Performance of the Pre-reform Tax System

Comprehensive reform of any tax structure begins with a thorough evaluation of the performance of the existing system. What is to be fixed? In the case of the Guatemalan system, there were four major problem areas:

1. Tax revenues were not adequate to support expenditure needs, and were not growing automatically in response to increases to GDP.
2. The rate of tax compliance was too low.
3. The distribution of tax burdens was perceived to be inequitable.
4. The tax system was not neutral with respect to economic choices, and this compromised the performance of the economy.

Revenue Adequacy

The test of fiscal adequacy in any country is a revenue yield that will match the budgeted level of expenditures. Based on the increasing size of the government deficit in the pre-reform period and the declining level of real per capita expenditures, one could say unequivocally that the Guatemalan government revenue system did not meet this test. Arguably more important is for the government to intervene where the market fails to provide an adequate level of public goods and to insure that the poor have access to at least a minimal level of public services. There is some evidence and plenty of conjecture about whether this test of good government has been met in Guatemala in the past. The Inter-American Development Bank (1991, p. 96) noted that "the tax burden and fiscal spending are being held quite low and are not adequate to meet some of the basic needs of the population."

Were revenues inordinately low in Guatemala? The most common barometer of revenue performance is the ratio of tax revenue to GDP. By world standards, this ratio has always been very low in Guatemala and fell to 6.9 percent in the 1990s, an amount practically unheard of anywhere in the world (Table 1.1). To estimate the extent to which Guatemalan tax levels were out of line with those in other countries, a comparative analysis of 66 developing economies was carried out. After controlling for the ease with which taxes could be raised in each of these countries (e.g., by controlling for the level of income, the level of industrialization, and the degree of openness of the economy to foreign trade), we concluded that Guatemala ranked 61st in tax effort. These results suggested that if Guatemala chose to exert an internationally average tax effort, it needed to double the 1990 level of taxes. A "normal" tax effort for Guatemala would be between 12 and 15 percent. Guatemala's actual collections have remained far below its "potential" for three reasons: tax rates were too low, tax bases were too narrow, and the compliance rate was too low.

To make matters worse, the tax effort situation seemed to deteriorate in the early 1990s. The revenue yield from *all* major taxes in the system was less responsive to income growth in 1989 and 1990 than in previous years. With the single exception of the business income tax, the same was true in 1988 as compared to 1987. In fact, for every 1 percent increase in GDP, tax revenues increased by only 0.18 percent in 1989 and 0.61 percent in 1990 (Table 2.1). The greater responsiveness in 1991 was due to discretionary, temporary changes. Revenue collections were lagging both population growth and inflation. In real per capita terms, tax revenues actually fell from $123 in 1988 to $63 in 1990 to $45 in 1993.

Why did the growth in tax revenue slow by more than the growth in GDP? The answer would appear to be some combination of reduced compliance, the generally poor performance of the economy, and the preferential tax treatment of certain sectors of the economy. Our analysis suggests exclusions from the tax base were the biggest problem. The amounts of revenue loss were not trivial. If the government had collected even the same share of GDP in taxes in 1990 as it did in 1988, revenues would have been Q640 million higher. This would not have fully covered the 1990 deficit of Q900 in the nonfinancial sector, but it would have made a significant contribution.

For whatever reason, between 1988 and 1990 there was a 20 percent decline in real revenues, and the outlook was for continuing decline. Absent discretionary changes to reverse this pattern or new external sources of funding, the ratio of taxes to GDP continued to fall, and the govern-

TABLE 2.1 GDP Elasticity of Revenue Collections[a]

	1985	1986	1987	1988	1989	1990	1991	1992
Total Current Revenues	1.65	1.52	2.69	1.48	0.32	0.36	1.72	1.73
Less: Non-tax Revenues	2.29	0.88	2.70	1.19	0.86	-0.51	5.01	0.53
Equals: Tax Revenues	1.46	1.75	2.69	1.56	0.18	0.61	1.15	1.73
Income Taxes	2.08	1.37	4.04	4.07	-0.13	0.56	2.46	-0.24
Individuals	1.27	1.03	3.16	2.13	-1.60	0.48	2.41	0.41
Businesses	2.55	1.54	4.42	4.82	0.31	0.58	2.47	-0.37
Value-Added Tax	2.79	1.05	2.84	1.28	0.81	0.95	0.80	2.63
Customs Duties	-0.02	1.74	8.47	2.62	0.28	0.65	0.68	5.22
Excise Taxes	0.63	0.43	3.48	0.42	-0.06	0.72	1.14	1.93
Export Taxes	-3.60	49.18	-2.47	-1.99	-3.14	-2.08	-1.50	-3.83
All Other	3.34	0.58	2.03	1.35	1.12	-0.02	0.24	1.83

[a]Not adjusted for discretionary changes.

Source: Ministry of Finance, Government of Guatemala, as reported to *Consultoria Para La Administracion Fiscal*, Policy Economics Group, KPMG Peat Marwick, and Policy Research Program, Georgia State University, 1991-1993.

ment faced the hard choice of slowing expenditure growth or turning more heavily to inflationary sources of finance.

Compliance

A low rate of compliance and lax enforcement are often cited as major problems with the Guatemalan tax system. The evidence to back up these charges is limited because there is no easy way to measure changes in compliance with the tax system. Indicators of changes in the gap between expected and actual tax collections, however, provide some evidence in support of the proposition that the compliance rate has deteriorated.

The first is indirect evidence: the tax share of GDP declined between 1988 and 1990 for all taxes, and for each tax in the system. One could not argue that this was due to an inherently income-inelastic tax system because the individual income tax had a progressive rate, the value-added tax was not unusually narrow-based, and excises were levied on an ad valorem basis. Moreover, all of these taxes had shown an income-elastic response in earlier years. Income elasticity was greater than unity in every year between 1985 and 1988. Nor were there discretionary changes that reduced the tax share of national income. A declining compliance rate is a more reasonable explanation.

The second piece of evidence was obtained in a more direct manner. KPMG developed a model to estimate the amount of additional revenue due in each year,[1] and compared this estimated amount with the change in actual collections.[2] If the change in actual collections fell short of the estimated amounts, this was referred to as an increase in the "compliance gap." If actuals exceeded the estimates, the situation was one of overcompliance (e.g., collection of arrears). The results of this analysis (presented in Table 2.2) show that the compliance gap for the business tax was equivalent to about 7 percent in 1990 but turned to a 12 percent overcompliance in 1991. In the case of the individual income tax, the rate of noncompliance was about 13 percent in 1990, but fell back to less than 3 percent in 1991. Compliance with the value-added tax (VAT) seemed to deteriorate in 1991, but was reasonably strong in 1990. Though such estimates are subject to error, in particular we have not been able to eliminate the effects of the amnesty and the one-time business assessment in 1990-1991. Moreover, the model only takes account of those individuals and firms who were filers in 1988. These problems notwithstanding, we read these results as being consistent with the claim that there was a decline in the compliance rate over the 1989-1991 period. Note, however, that these percentages represent *changes* from the 1988 level, not estimates of the overall compliance rate.

TABLE 2.2 Estimated Change in Compliance (in Millions of Quetzales)

	Business Income Tax	Individual Income Tax	Value- Added Tax	Alcohol/ Tobacco Excises
Tax Year: 1989				
Reported Change in Liability	Q270	Q100	Q558	Q118
Estimated Change in Liability	261	98	577	118
Difference	+9	+2	-19	0
Difference as a Percentage of Estimated Liability	+3.4%	+2.0%	-3.3%	0
Tax Year: 1990				
Reported Change in Liability	Q318	Q124	Q792	Q150
Estimated Change in Liability	342	143	795	157
Difference	-24	-19	-3	-7
Difference as a Percentage of Estimated Liability	-7.0%	-13.3%	-0.4%	-4.5%
Tax Year: 1991				
Reported Change in Liability	Q537	Q170	Q1047	Q187
Estimated Change in Liability	478	175	1121	178
Difference	+59	-5	-74	+9
Difference as a Percentage of Estimated Liability	+12.3%	-2.9%	-6.6%	+5.1%

Source: Ministry of Finance, Government of Guatemala, as reported to *Consultoria Para La Administracion Fiscal*, Policy Economics Group, KPMG Peat Marwick, and Policy Research Program, Georgia State University, 1991-1993.

The policy-relevant question is why compliance rates have fallen. There are several possible explanations in Guatemala but little evidence to help us sort out their relative importance:

• Enforcement efforts were unusually weak in an election year.

- The tax administration was inefficient, e.g., collection procedures were such that some tax liabilities went uncollected, the auditing system did not pick up unpaid liabilities, etc.
- Tax evasion was not discouraged, either because the enforcement was not strict enough or the penalties were too light.
- Taxpayers resisted payment because the compliance costs were too high.
- Taxpayers resisted payment because they did not believe that the government delivered services commensurate with the taxes paid, or because they felt that the tax system was not applied evenly to all taxpayers.

The Distribution of Tax Burdens

There is a perception that the Guatemalan tax system is unfair.[3] Some observers and analysts simply assume that the very unequal distribution of income in Guatemala is partly a result of a regressive tax system. Others argue that the poor are burdened more than are middle- and upper-income families because there is a heavy reliance on indirect taxes. Some see the tax system as unfair because it offers special treatment to certain businesses and families. It is argued that the administration of the system and the laws are biased enough that even persons of the same income level were treated differently, and some businesses felt that they were taxed more heavily than others. To address these perceptions of unfairness, tax burdens were estimated for Guatemalan households with different income levels, and effective tax rates were estimated for different sectors of the economy for both the company income tax and the VAT.

Vertical Equity

One way to assess the equity, or fairness, of a tax system is to ask whether there is a correspondence between the ability to pay taxes (usually measured by income or wealth) and the actual distribution of tax burdens. But what kind of correspondence is equitable? Some argue for proportional taxation—a system in which everyone pays about the same share of income in taxes. Others argue for progressivity, i.e., the effective tax rate should rise with income. In fact, one cannot say that progressivity or proportionality in a tax system is good or not good. It depends on the national view about how much income inequality is acceptable and about the role that the tax system should play in reducing this inequality.

As may be seen from the data presented in the third column of Table

2.3, the distribution of income in Guatemala was highly unequal, with the wealthiest 10 percent of families earning more than half of all income, and the wealthiest 1 percent earning about one-fourth of all income. This was one of the more dramatic cases of income inequality in the world, and would seem to make the case for progressive taxation. However fair taxing higher-income families more heavily seemed, it was not clear that taxation could effectively reduce the skewness in the income distribution. For one thing, taxes, including payroll taxes, constituted no more than 10 percent of total output in Guatemala, hence the potential for using the tax system to redistribute income was quite limited. Anyway, more progressive tax systems give greater incentives to evasion and avoidance, and these tend to be successful strategies of tax reduction in low-income countries where the administrative systems are not well developed. Another consideration was that income redistribution might be more effectively accomplished on the expenditure side of the budget, and in any case the real issue was *fiscal* incidence (the net effect of the distribution of tax burdens and expenditure benefits) and not *tax* incidence. The point here is that taxation is only one of a number of government policies that affect the distribution of income and is not necessarily the most effective policy.

Galper and Ramos' (1992) analysis of the vertical equity of the Guatemalan tax system concludes that in the pre-reform period, the system was in fact progressive, i.e., the effective tax rate rose consistently with household income. The lowest 10 percent of income earners paid 7.2 to 7.8 percent of their income in taxes, and the top decile of families paid over 11 percent. The disaggregation of the top income bracket indicates that there is further progression among top decile households, and the wealthiest 1 percent face an effective tax rate of 12.1 percent. The progressivity in the overall tax system is due to the fact that the highest income group (1) participates in the individual income tax; (2) is a heavier consumer of taxable commodities; and (3) owns capital, hence shares disproportionately in the burden of the company income tax and indirect taxes on investment goods.

These findings concerning the distribution of tax burdens across income classes provide two interesting insights about the vertical equity of the pre-reform Guatemalan tax system. The first is that it was not regressive, and it may well have been slightly progressive. The second is that the tax system did reach down (through indirect taxes) to cover low-income Guatemalans. In fact, the poorest families appeared to bear a slightly higher burden than those in the middle-income range. The latter point seems to refute the idea that Guatemalan taxes were paid by only a select few. The data in Table 2.3 show that households in the bottom five income deciles earned 10 percent of the income and paid 11.4 percent

TABLE 2.3 Distribution of Tax Burdens by Income Class, 1992 Levels of Economic Activity: Pre-Reform System

Household Income Class (in Quetzales)	Percentage of Households	Percentage of Income	Taxes as a Percentage of Income							
			Individual Income	Social Security	Corporate Income Tax	Value-Added Tax	Customs Duties	Excise Taxes	Other	Total
Under Q2,465	9.9%	0.6%	0.0%	3.0%	1.8%	0.8%	0.5%	1.0%	0.0%	7.2%
Q2,465 - 3,750	10.0	1.3	0.0	2.9	1.7	0.9	0.5	1.0	0.1	7.1
Q3,750 - 5,250	10.0	1.9	0.0	2.9	1.6	1.2	0.7	1.0	0.1	7.5
Q5,250 - 7,250	10.0	2.6	0.0	2.7	1.5	1.5	0.9	1.1	0.1	7.8
Q7,250 - 9,450	10.0	3.6	0.0	2.2	1.1	1.5	0.9	1.1	0.1	6.8
Q9,450 - 12,700	10.1	4.7	0.0	2.8	1.4	2.0	1.2	1.1	0.1	8.6
Q12,700 - 17,600	10.0	6.4	0.0	2.5	1.2	2.4	1.4	1.3	0.1	8.9
Q17,600 - 25,550	10.0	8.9	0.0	2.4	1.2	2.7	1.6	1.4	0.1	9.4
Q25,550 - 43,250	10.0	13.9	0.0	1.9	0.9	3.1	1.9	1.6	0.2	9.7
Q43,250 and Over	10.0	56.0	1.0	0.9	1.9	3.1	2.3	1.6	0.4	11.2
Q43,250 - 74,450	5.1	12.0	0.1	1.1	0.6	3.5	2.2	1.8	0.3	9.6
Q74,450 - 230,000	3.9	20.1	0.6	1.1	1.5	3.3	2.3	1.9	0.4	11.1
Q230,000 and Over	1.0	24.0	1.7	0.7	2.8	2.7	2.3	1.4	0.5	12.1
Total	100.0	100.0	0.5	1.5	1.6	2.8	1.9	1.5	0.3	10.2

*The household distribution roughly represents income deciles. Based on household income levels for tax year 1992 (July 1991 to June 1992). Distributions may not sum to exactly 100 percent due to rounding.

Source: Harvey Galper and Fernando Ramos, *The Incidence of Guatemalan Taxes,* Technical Memorandum No. 32. Guatemala Fiscal Administration Project. Atlanta: Georgia State University, College of Business Administration, Policy Research Center; Washington DC: KPMG Peat Marwick Policy Economics Group.

of the taxes. The conclusion we draw from Galper and Ramo's empirical analysis is that it would be hard to lay heavy blame for Guatemala's unequal income distribution on a regressive tax system.

Horizontal Equity

Another dimension of fairness in taxation is horizontal equity. The issue here is whether individuals and families in the same circumstances are treated equally under the tax system, and whether the tax structure favors one kind of business activity over another. Ideally, a system should offer all individuals and businesses the same treatment under the tax system (except in cases where there is a deliberate intention to encourage or discourage a particular kind of activity or to subsidize a particular kind of business or household). If the tax system is not horizontally equitable, confidence in the system will be undermined, and taxpayers will resist payment by avoidance schemes or by outright evasion.

The Guatemalan individual income tax in the pre-reform period was not horizontally equitable. Because interest income (and effectively, capital gains) were not taxed, people at the same income level were treated differently, depending on how they earned their income. A similar problem with preferential treatment arose with respect to the self-employed (who were largely outside the tax net) and those receiving tax-free bonus income.

Horizontal equity is also a goal in the taxation of businesses. Different businesses shift taxes in different proportions to consumers, labor, or owners; therefore, differential tax treatment of businesses has implications for the horizontal equity of the system. It also has implications for the investment and resource allocation decisions of businesses. Was the pre-reform Guatemalan system neutral or characterized by horizontal inequities in business taxation? Evaluation of the horizontal fairness of the system depends on how one defines "an equally situated firm." The variation in effective company income tax rates[4] for different (nonfinancial) sectors of the economy is shown in the right column of Table 2.4. The variation among those who paid was fairly uniform in 1992. However, these data do not include the considerable number of firms with zero tax liability, and therein lies the major source of the horizonal equity problem.

The horizontal equity of the value-added tax is estimated with the computations reported in Tables 2.5 and 2.6. As may be seen in the last

TABLE 2.4 Distribution of Business Income Tax Liability by Industry: 1992

Industry[a]	Tax Returns		Adjusted Taxable Income		Tax Liability (after credits)		
	Number	Percentage of Total	Amount (Q millions)	Percentage of Total	Amount (Q millions)	Percentage of Total	Tax as Percentage of Adjusted Net Income
Agriculture, Forestry, Hunting, Fishing	925	6.6%	99	6.5%	32	6.4%	32.3%
Mining & Petroleum	58	0.4	28	1.8	10	2.0	35.7
Manufacturing Industries	2,057	14.7	513	33.6	171	34.1	33.3
Electricity, Gas & Water	28	0.2	64	4.2	22	4.4	34.4
Construction	530	3.8	28	1.8	9	1.8	32.1
Commerce: Wholesale, Retail; Restaurants, Hotels	4,341	31.1	509	33.3	168	33.5	33.0
Transportation, Storage & Communication	441	3.2	66	4.3	22	4.4	33.3
Finance & Insurance	2,194	15.7	121	7.9	38	7.6	31.4
Community, Social & Personal Services	1,408	10.1	51	3.3	16	3.2	31.4
Not Classified	1,984	14.2	49	3.2	14	2.8	28.6
Total	13,971	100.0	1,527	100.0	501	100.0	32.8

[a]Financial institutions are not included. Listing includes businesses with positive adjusted effective taxable income.
Source: Ministry of Finance, Government of Guatemala, as reported to Consultoria Para La Administracion Fiscal, Policy Economics Group, KPMG Peat Marwick, and Policy Research Program, Georgia State University, 1991-1993.

TABLE 2.5 Value-Added Tax Base on Domestic Transactions: 1992 Levels of Economic Activity

	Total Sales (Q millions)	Percentage of Total Sales Reported on VAT Returns	Percentage of Reported Sales Taxed at 27 Percent	VAT as a Percentage of Total Sales
Agriculture	Q14,504	53.0%	24.9%	0.9%
Forestry	1,966	4.1	57.8	0.2
Mining	682	93.2	27.8	1.8
Food Products	4,920	87.0	68.4	4.2
Sugar	1,281	93.2	6.4	0.4
Textiles	2,255	93.2	62.5	4.0
Wood Products	451	37.4	75.0	2.0
Paper Products	2,316	91.0	44.1	2.8
Chemical	3,746	93.2	52.6	3.4
Petroleum Products	3,723	88.8	4.4	0.3
Minerals	541	93.2	71.0	4.6
Cement	612	93.2	87.0	5.7
Metals	1,487	93.2	63.6	4.1
Other Industries	2,593	18.5	72.2	0.9
Electricity/Water	954	20.3	85.7	5.6
Construction	2,821	26.6	47.1	0.9
Commerce	76,403	19.1	69.3	0.9
Transportation/ Communication	6,464	60.2	73.3	3.1
Finance	9,214	13.2	62.4	0.6
Services	12,302	25.1	81.1	1.4
Total	149,232	34.7	54.7	1.4

Source: Ministry of Finance, Government of Guatemala, as reported to *Consultoria Para La Administracion Fiscal*, Policy Economics Group, KPMG Peat Marwick, and Policy Research Program, Georgia State University, 1991-1993.

column of Table 2.5, the variation across sectors in the ratio of value-added tax to total sales was quite wide. Of course, some of this variation was due to sectoral differences in the value-added tax. But part of the variation was due to the substantial differences in the amounts of total sales that were fully taxed (Columns 2 and 3 of Table 2.5), a result of some combination of zero rating, exemptions, and unregistered firms. In total, two-thirds of domestic sales value was outside the tax base,[5] and only about half of that amount was taxed at the full 7 percent. The VAT, therefore, turned out to be equivalent to a 1.4 percent tax on domestic sales and a 5 percent tax on the duty-paid value of imports.

TABLE 2.6 Tax Base on International Trade: 1992 Levels of Economic Activity[a]

	Value of Imports (Q millions)	Import Duty Percent Dutiable	VAT Revenue as Percentage of Import Value	As Percentage of Duty-Inclusive Import Value
Agriculture	Q322	56.5%	2.7%	2.6%
Forestry	3	32.4	7.1	6.9
Mining	699	88.0	0.4	0.4
Food Products	602	61.3	6.1	5.7
Sugar	0	0.0	0.0	0.0
Textiles	560	59.5	7.5	7.0
Wood Products	20	35.7	7.4	6.8
Paper Products	416	64.3	6.5	6.0
Chemical	2,389	81.0	7.5	7.0
Petroleum Products	758	24.9	2.3	2.2
Minerals	102	91.3	7.9	6.9
Cement	57	97.7	6.7	6.0
Metals	964	81.1	7.5	6.9
Other Industries	3,226	81.0	7.2	6.5
Electricity/Water	0	0.0	0.0	0.0
Construction	0	0.0	0.0	0.0
Commerce	0	0.0	0.0	0.0
Transportation/ Communication	1,079	0.0	0.0	0.0
Finance	100	0.0	0.0	0.0
Service	675	0.0	0.0	0.0
Total	11,970	62.2	5.3	5.0

[a]Less than Q500,000.

Source: Ministry of Finance, Government of Guatemala, as reported to *Consultoria Para La Administracion Fiscal*, Policy Economics Group, KPMG Peat Marwick, and Policy Research Program, Georgia State University, 1991-1993.

Notes

1. The model used by KPMG is based on financial data drawn from a random sample of firms. A tax calculator was developed to estimate the amount of revenue due in each year, adjusted for timing of payments and assuming "current" rates of compliance. For the individual income tax, the estimate of this amount (collections-based liability) is Q98 million in 1989. The reported liability for the individual income tax in 1989 was Q100 million (See Table 2.2), hence the estimate from the model is reasonably accurate (about 2 percent short of actual liability in 1989). For the same year, actual business tax collections were Q9

million or 3.4 percent less than estimated liability. Similar estimates for 1990 and 1991 are reported in Table 2.2.

2. The microsimulation models used by KPMG are described in Martinez-Vasquez, et al. (1989); Newland and Beckwith (1992a); and Greaney, et al. (1992a).

3. This section draws heavily on Galper and Ramos (1992).

4. The ratio of tax to "economic" income. The latter is derived by adjusting taxable income to include interest income, bad debt deductions, and depletion allowances.

5. Much of the exclusion from the VAT base was in the commerce and services area. If these two sectors are excluded from the computation, only one-third of domestic sales was outside the VAT base.

3

Problems with the Guatemalan Tax System

No country can fully satisfy the norms for "the good tax system" as laid down in classical economics. It is important, however, to consider these norms as a starting point in thinking about the deficiencies of the Guatemalan system. The basic principles describing the good tax system might be stated as follows:

- Its yield should be adequate to cover planned expenditure and should be reasonably certain over time.
- It should be administrable at reasonable cost, and it should not impose large compliance costs.
- It should be understandable to taxpayers.
- It should conform to some commonly held notions of fairness in the distribution of tax burdens.
- It should not interfere with market decisions, except to correct some undesirable distortion that the market will not correct.

There are three broad areas where the tax system in Guatemala system departed substantially from these norms and from the objectives of government policy: the level of taxes was inadequate to support desired expenditures; the many exclusions from the tax base compromised the fairness and revenue yield of the system, and led to distortions of economic choices; and the tax administration was deficient.

The Level of Taxes

It is important to emphasize that there is no definitive way to state how high taxes *should* be in any country. This is a political decision that reflects how the country wants to divide its resources between publicly and privately provided goods and services. But there are two ways in which it may be argued that taxes were too low in Guatemala. The first is by examination of the budgetary shortfall, and the second is by comparison with international practice.

Taxes and the Deficit

The first approach to judging the adequacy of tax effort of a country is to consider the level and persistence of the fiscal deficit. The premise is that a continuing deficit is prima facie evidence that revenues collected are not enough to cover the amount the country wants to spend. The overall central government deficit in Guatemala (including nonfinancial public enterprise and central bank losses) hovered around 4.5 percent of GDP during the 1980s.

The level of taxes was not sufficient to cover the amount of expenditures that the Guatemalan government chose to make. In fiscal 1990, the central government fiscal (nonfinancial sector) deficit was over Q800 million (about 2.5 percent of GDP), and the consolidated deficit was on the order of Q1.6 billion (about 4.7 percent of GDP). By world standards these are not large numbers, and many countries face larger deficits. However, Guatemala has such a small public sector that covering even a modest deficit required major fiscal adjustments. The following assumptions will give some idea of the magnitude of the tax changes required to balance the budget:

- If the 1990 central government deficit were to be fully covered by an increase in taxation, the increment in total taxes would have to be 44 percent in one year. If the entire increase were to be funded by the value-added tax as levied under the pre-reform system, the tax rate would have to increase from 7 percent to nearly 15 percent.
- If the *consolidated* deficit were to be covered, the required increase in taxes would be nearly 90 percent, and the required increase in the VAT rate would rise to 21 percent.
- If the deficit were to be met by expenditure reduction, per capita expenditures would fall from Q335 to Q241 to cover the central government shortfall, and to Q165 to cover the total deficit.

In contrast to previous years, in 1991 the nonfinancial public sector balance showed a surplus of 0.4 percent of GDP, and the overall deficit (including central bank losses) was down to 1.2 percent of GDP. It remained at about 1 percent of GDP in 1992.

Deficit numbers alone cannot be used to justify a tax reform and define its objectives. In 1990 Guatemala's fiscal deficit seemed to call for a significant tax increase, but by 1992 the fiscal deficit had diminished significantly. Some in Guatemala read this improvement in fiscal position as negating any need for a reform. However, the improved fiscal position resulted from a forced bond placement, a public sector payroll reduction, and a substantial increase in utility rates. One could not count on a repeat of these measures in every year. It would be difficult to argue that Guatemala had reached an equilibrium in its fiscal sector in 1992.

International Comparisons

The question of adequacy of taxes might be approached in another way: Are a country's taxes out of line with those in "similarly situated" countries? One could ask this question for at least two reasons. If there is an international norm for the level of taxes raised by developing countries, one wants to know if the country under study is near this norm. If the level of taxes in a country is too low relative to other countries, it might suggest that an adequate level of public services is not being provided, that the tax system is not playing a "normal" role in income redistribution, or that inadequate infrastructure is available to support economic development. If taxes are too high, it might suggest a noncompetitive position in attracting investment, i.e., high taxes might reduce the rate of return to investors. International comparisons also have value in showing how much a country's level of taxation can change without bringing it out of line with the rest of the world.

Here, we take two quite different approaches to the estimation of Guatemalan tax effort. The first uses a regression technique to estimate the capacity to raise taxes in a sample of countries and then compares estimated capacity to actual collections. The second approach calculates the capacity to raise revenue from each major tax and then aggregates the results to obtain an estimate of tax effort. The two approaches, the regression method and the representative tax system method, are described in Bahl (1971, 1972) and are well critiqued in Bird (1976).

The Regression Approach. The dependent variable to be explained in this approach is taxable capacity, measured as the ratio of tax revenue to GDP (i.e., the "tax ratio"). A variety of proxies for "tax handles" are used as independent variables in this equation. These variables are meant to capture the effects of differences in economic structure on the ability to raise tax revenue. For example:

- A higher level of per capita GNP suggests a greater ability to raise taxes.

- A larger import and export sector means that tax collection will be easier.
- If more people live in cities, and less GDP is generated in the agricultural sector, the tax system will be more revenue productive.

From a regression equation, an estimated value of the tax ratio $(\hat{T}_y)$ is obtained, i.e., the amount that this country "could" collect by international standards. The level of tax effort (E) is the ratio of the actual to the estimated tax ratio, i.e.,

$$E = T_y \setminus \hat{T}_y$$

This analysis updates the results of Lotz and Morss (1967), Bahl (1971), and Chelliah, Baas and Kelly (1975).[1] The general form for these specifications is as follows:

Lotz-Morss:	$T_y = a + bY_p + cXM_y$
Bahl:	$T_y = a + bN_y + cA_y$
Chelliah, Baas and Kelly	$T_y = a + b\,(Y_p - X_p) + cN_y + dX'_y$

where:

T_y	=	ratio of taxes (excluding social security contributions) to GDP
Y_p	=	per capita GNP (in U.S. dollars)
XM_y	=	ratio of the sum of exports plus imports to GNP
N_y	=	share of mining in GDP (including petroleum)
A_y	=	share of agriculture in GDP
$(Y_p - X_p)$	=	per capita non-export income (in U.S. dollars) and
X'_y	=	ratio of non-mineral exports to GNP.

We re-estimated these equations with ordinary least squares, using cross-section data for thirty-three developing countries for the years 1981-1986. The data were taken from the International Monetary Fund's *International Financial Statistics Yearbook* and *Government Finance Statistics Yearbook*, and from the United Nations' *Yearbook of National Accounts Statistics, 1986.*

The index of tax effort is produced by dividing the actual tax ratio by the expected tax ratio for each of the three specifications estimated (Table 3.1).[2] The results show that Guatemala ranks 61st among the 66 countries in the level of tax effort. By these three specifications of the tax-effort model, Guatemala's tax effort is 55.5 percent, 41.6 percent, and 46.5

TABLE 3.1 Estimated Tax Effort Rankings and Indexes: Regression Approach

	Rank[a]	Index[a]	Rank[b]	Index[b]	Rank[c]	Index[c]
Indonesia	1	226.4	23	116.0	16	129.2
Israel	2	209.9	1	277.6	3	194.6
Hungary	3	182.0	2	226.0	4	186.8
Guyana	4	158.2	4	206.2	1	212.8
Ethiopia	5	153.2	11	146.5	8	151.1
Tanzania	6	145.9	7	152.1	15	131.8
Chile	7	144.0	30	105.7	10	146.6
So. Africa	8	139.1	21	119.6	20	118.4
Jamaica	9	136.0	10	147.2	9	150.4
Tunisia	10	135.8	18	128.7	12	143.3
Morocco	11	131.5	26	107.2	13	134.7
Zambia	12	131.3	20	120.7	6	156.3
Cameroon	13	130.0	34	100.9	34	101.0
Togo	14	127.3	6	159.5	5	161.8
Yeman Arab Rep.	15	126.9	29	105.7	7	151.1
Sri Lanka	16	123.0	19	121.4	17	128.2
Congo	17	120.2	8	150.4	11	143.6
India	18	119.9	48	75.0	38	95.3
Mexico	19	119.7	45	80.0	29	103.7
Venezuela	20	118.7	31	102.1	22	115.8
Fiji	21	113.6	22	116.7	19	118.8
Benin	22	113.4	32	102.0	33	101.2
Uruguay	23	107.0	46	79.3	40	89.8
Peru	24	106.8	3	209.6	2	197.6
Suriname	25	105.2	28	105.9	25	110.4
Liberia	26	104.4	12	144.3	18	119.5
Malawi	27	104.2	16	131.1	23	113.4
Ecuador	28	103.0	44	80.5	42	89.5
Senegal	29	100.9	25	112.4	26	109.0
Thailand	30	98.2	43	81.4	39	90.9
Panama	31	97.6	47	75.5	36	98.6
Gambia	32	97.5	27	106.7	24	11.3
Malaysia	33	97.4	14	138.7	14	132.0
Barbados	34	92.5	24	115.4	32	102.9
Pakistan	35	92.4	60	47.0	50	68.3
El Salvador	36	92.3	49	72.4	45	85.8
Papua N. Guinea	37	91.8	13	142.8	21	117.2
Brazil	38	91.3	54	56.8	54	107.4
Solomon Is.	39	91.3	5	193.9	37	96.1
Burkina Faso	40	89.8	33	101.8	35	99.0
Belize	41	88.9	9	148.7	27	107.5
St. Vincent	42	87.0	17	130.7	31	103.7
Mauritius	43	84.4	36	97.4	41	89.8
Korea	44	83.6	41	83.7	44	86.9
Ghana	45	83.0	40	87.5	48	73.9
Mali	46	82.6	15	134.4	43	89.5

(continues)

TABLE 3.1 (*continued*)

	Rank[a]	Index[a]	Rank[b]	Index[b]	Rank[c]	Index[c]
Costa Rica	47	81.9	38	90.8	52	64.8
Argentina	48	79.0	56	56.7	*	*
Phillipines	49	78.2	50	64.4	49	71.0
Nepal	50	75.5	39	90.0	54	63.1
Colombia	51	74.6	58	51.9	30	103.7
Cyprus	52	73.0	42	82.5	46	83.8
Dominican Rep.	53	71.9	57	53.2	51	65.7
Maldives	54	68.5	35	100.5	*	*
Malta	55	67.9	37	91.5	47	82.2
Bolivia	56	63.6	59	47.7	57	54.4
Yugoslavia	57	63.2	55	56.8	55	60.2
Syrian Arab Rep.	58	62.0	52	60.1	53	64.2
Bangladesh	59	58.7	51	62.1	56	55.1
Paraguay	60	57.0	61	45.7	58	49.9
Guatemala	**61**	**55.5**	**62**	**41.6**	**59**	**46.5**
Iran	62	42.0	63	35.3	61	33.0
Oman	63	38.1	53	58.2	60	39.6
Sierra Leone	64	32.4	64	30.4	62	24.3
Bahrain	65	11.9	65	24.8	63	23.1
Kuwait	66	7.1	66	13.6	64	8.1

[a]Lotz, Jorgen, and Elliot Morss, "Measuring Tax Effort in Developing Countries," *International Monetary Fund Staff Papers* 14.3 (Nov. 1967): 478-499.

[b]Bahl, Roy, "A Regression Approach to Tax Effort and Tax Ratio Analysis," *International Monetary Fund Staff Papers* 18.3 (Nov. 1971): 570-612.

[c]Chelliah "Trends in Taxation in Developing Countries," *International Monetary Fund Staff Papers* 18.3 (Nov. 1971): 570-612.

*Not included.

Source: Estimated by authors with data from *Government Finance Statistics* (1994) and *International Financial Statistics* (1994), as reported in Roy Bahl, Jorge Martinez-Vazquez, Michael Jordan, and Sally Wallace. 1993. "Intercountry Comparisons of Fiscal Performance." Technical Note No. 7. Guatemala Fiscal Administration Project. Atlanta: Georgia State University, College of Business Administration, Policy Research Center; Washington, DC: KPMG Peat Marwick Policy Economics Group.

percent of the international average. A "normal" tax effort for Guatemala during this period would have been between 12 and 15 percent of GDP. Hence, one can conclude from the regression approach that if Guatemala wanted to exert an internationally average tax effort, nearly twice the level of taxes would have been required. These results also show that Guatemala's tax effort was well below the average for all Latin American countries in the sample and below that for other Central American countries in the sample.

The Representative Tax System Approach[3]. An alternative approach to measuring tax effort takes account of the capacity to collect each tax. The question asked is this: If a country levied its present tax structure, but at international average tax rates, what total level of tax revenues could be expected? A comparison of this expectation to actual collections gives an index of effort for each tax and, with aggregation, for the tax system. To calculate the average tax rate for each type of tax, we estimate regressions for each tax where the level of revenue is expressed as a function of the tax base and control variables. We follow this representative tax system approach to measuring tax effort (Bahl 1972), and use the following categorization of taxes:

Personal income taxes (including payroll taxes but not social security taxes)
Corporate income taxes
Property taxes (including motor vehicle taxes)
Internal indirect taxes (sales, excise, other internal indirect taxes)
Import taxes
Export taxes
Other taxes (IMF definition)[4]

For each of these taxes, a proxy tax base is developed to reflect intercountry variations in the true tax base. A proxy base is used because data can be gathered from published sources, whereas data on actual tax bases are not available.

Personal income taxes and internal indirect taxes are assumed to be taxes on incomes generated in the monetized sector, that is, on incomes generated outside the subsistence sector. The incomes of the monetized sector are proxied by deducting the agricultural share of GDP from total GDP and adding back the agricultural share of exports. Because there seems no preferable, measurable alternative, total GDP is assumed to be the proxy base for property taxes. The value of commodity imports is assumed to be the proxy base for import taxes. The GDP is assumed to be the base for other taxes. The proxy base for corporate income taxes is assumed to be GDP generated in the mining and manufacturing sectors plus the agricultural share of exports; and the proxy base for export taxes is the value of commodity exports.

Various authors have noted that policy with respect to government expenditure and taxation among developing countries depends on the level of per capita income (Tanzi 1987; Heller and Diamond 1990), and we have used dummy variables to reflect this possibility. We have assigned a value of 1 to the dummy variable if the country's per capita income exceeds $400 and a value of 0 if it is less than or equal to $400.

Based on this specification of tax categories, proxy tax bases and the exogenous economic variables, the following regression equations were estimated:

lnPERS	=	$b_{01} + b_{11} * ln\text{YVAR} + b_{21} * yp\text{DUM}$
lnCORP	=	$b_{02} + b_{12} * ln\text{NVAR} + b_{22} * yp\text{DUM}$
lnSALES	=	$b_{03} + b_{13} * ln\text{YVAR} + b_{23} * yp\text{DUM}$
lnPROP	=	$b_{04} + b_{14} * ln\text{GDP} + b_{24} * yp\text{DUM}$
lnEXP	=	$b_{05} + b_{15} * ln\text{COMEXP} + b_{25} * yp\text{DUM}$
lnIM	=	$b_{06} + b_{16} * ln\text{COMIMP} + b_{26} * yp\text{DUM}$
lnOH	=	$b_{07} + b_{17} * ln\text{YVAR} + b_{27} * yp\text{DUM}$

where

ypDUM	=	the dummy variable for per capita income, = 1 if per capita income is greater than \$400, 0 if it is less than \$400,
lnPERS	=	the natural logarithm of revenues collected from personal income taxes,
lnCORP	=	the natural logarithm of revenues collected from corporate income taxes,
lnSALES	=	the natural logarithm of revenues collected from sales, excise and other indirect internal taxes, excluding motor vehicle taxes,
lnPROP	=	the natural logarithm of revenues collected from property taxes, including motor vehicle taxes,
lnEXP	=	the natural logarithm of revenues collected from export taxes,
lnIMP	=	the natural logarithm of revenues collected from import taxes,
lnYVAR	=	the natural logarithm of total GDP minus the agricultural share of GDP plus the agricultural share of exports,
lnNVAR	=	the natural logarithm of the mining and manufacturing share of GDP plus the agricultural share of exports,
lnGDP	=	the natural logarithm of GDP,
lnCOMEXP	=	the natural logarithm of the value of commodity exports, and
lnCOMIMP	=	the natural logarithm of the value of commodity imports.

The coefficients of the regression equations were used to calculate the average tax rates for each tax.[5] These rates were applied to the tax base for each tax for each country to estimate the expected levels of the various types of taxes for that country. The ratio of the actual amount of revenue from each source to the estimated amount from each source indicates the degree to which that source has been utilized compared to what is obtained from that source by the average country.

The results of this analysis, presented in Table 3.2, show that Guate-

TABLE 3.2 Estimated Tax Effort Indexes: Representative Tax System (Average = 100)

	All Taxes	Individual Income	Corporate Income	Sales	Property	Export	Import	Other
Israel	347.7	1111.8	287.7	370.2	502.8	0	59.7	124.0
Hungary	265.6	97.9	474.9	331.0	1289.7	0	73.2	1519.6
Guyana	214.1	190.6	465.6	596.3	337.7	49.3	58.6	43.4
Tanzania	203.1	187.3	697.3	267.2	68.7	6.0	52.3	980.0
Congo	194.7	158.1	571.0	99.9	7.5	16.9	99.9	102.2
Jamaica	188.9	240.3	242.1	419.1	295.2	0	26.3	351.1
Indonesia	188.8	57.4	682.7	62.4	116.6	56.0	45.5	107.2
Tunisia	184.4	138.7	157.6	174.9	367.2	109.4	210.0	265.5
Ethiopia	184.1	198.9	659.0	139.1	175.6	636.0	87.8	405.3
Togo	174.5	95.6	559.4	204.4	93.5	379.3	123.1	14.9
Suriname	172.3	238.1	252.7	67.8	308.4	597.2	144.3	109.7
Chile	168.9	130.1	111.7	206.4	190.5	0	76.3	1167.6
Peru	168.1	93.2	194.2	313.1	569.2	473.2	68.2	498.5
Liberia	165.6	283.5	86.2	227.4	116.3	8.6	135.0	96.5
Barbados	165.0	152.5	491.0	219.2	582.7	21.0	60.4	581.0
South Africa	164.4	387.7	261.6	115.9	220.3	22.5	31.3	251.7
Yemen Arab Republic	159.6	92.6	126.6	51.6	246.7	8.7	199.7	935.3
Cameroon	158.2	89.6	387.7	61.8	148.4	599.1	170.8	86.1
Morocco	157.8	126.5	109.2	206.8	285.4	186.0	101.0	565.7
Venezuela	157.5	99.0	603.6	21.0	113.8	0	277.6	74.1
Zambia	156.0	231.1	225.9	216.3	39.5	184.3	60.8	46.8
Fiji	152.8	314.1	149.7	94.8	98.4	0.1	126.0	50.7
Benin	151.3	97.2	410.9	68.3	49.8	118.8	209.6	295.7

(Continues)

TABLE 3.2 (Continued)

	All Taxes	Individual Income	Corporate Income	Sales	Property	Export	Import	Other
Senegal	137.8	154.1	74.2	189.1	185.4	56.6	128.2	34.8
Uruguay	137.4	37.6	41.6	221.6	305.8	174.3	128.4	294.7
Sri Lanka	136.9	66.9	229.3	147.3	184.6	262.1	102.9	0
Malaysia	134.9	122.4	260.6	74.2	438.0	895.2	74.3	292.6
Ghana	134.6	57.5	123.7	119.5	2.1	2932.4	128.3	4.6
Papua New Guinea	134.4	316.8	258.7	110.5	16.9	98.9	64.6	81.5
Panama	133.7	285.4	0	116.3	161.3	441.2	77.4	179.6
Nepal	133.0	61.6	76.1	172.9	209.5	37.2	134.1	50.4
Ecuador	125.8	61.3	302.2	55.5	98.0	89.0	162.4	57.9
Malawi	121.0	160.9	412.5	163.3	61.7	0	57.1	92.5
El Salvador	117.5	57.2	78.2	141.2	266.9	2654.8	41.9	21.5
Solomon Islands	117.5	154.6	90.9	24.0	27.9	869.2	111.9	13.5
Cyprus	113.7	189.6	65.4	118.3	499.3	0	70.5	248.0
Burkina Faso	112.7	98.0	215.6	110.6	47.8	75.8	96.9	1334.8
Belize	110.5	142.3	56.8	130.0	141.6	118.5	116.4	37.9
Gambia	108.3	80.5	136.3	43.3	35.8	88.7	140.2	40.7
Costa Rica	106.4	109.4	3.4	171.8	48.9	876.1	76.1	90.0
Korea	106.0	133.3	107.3	114.8	67.2	0	73.2	390.4
Thailand	105.8	90.7	67.6	122.0	98.6	193.3	108.6	73.9
Mali	104.3	84.8	101.4	174.0	165.2	163.4	45.9	2627.1
St. Vincent	103.4	129.5	84.2	141.4	126.4	80.8	99.2	49.0
Mauritius	97.3	67.4	54.5	76.3	300.8	143.7	110.6	75.9
Malta	92.3	273.7	356.6	36.4	425.5	0	61.1	126.2

Phillipines	91.2	78.3	75.5	86.6	119.2	187.0	113.8	149.5
Bolivia	91.0	5.8	9.5	172.2	18.6	528.4	106.4	22.0
Mexico	90.9	148.8	200.9	81.6	45.6	5.0	61.4	9.2
Dominican Republic	89.8	77.5	45.0	88.4	105.1	193.3	134.7	66.1
Syrian Arab Republic	85.0	162.2	0	27.2	351.2	245.8	86.7	640.8
Maldives	84.1	20.2	0	288.8	56.0	15.4	91.2	41.1
Argentina	83.8	16.9	0	88.1	142.2	757.0	159.0	1490.9
Pakistan	82.6	49.1	192.9	13.3	14.1	361.9	1431.6	1.9
India	81.1	91.7	145.5	49.5	55.2	22.1	380.4	0
Guatemala	**79.2**	**18.6**	**59.4**	**75.8**	**87.5**	**712.7**	**124.6**	**218.9**
Paraguay	79.2	4.8	87.1	84.6	317.5	41.5	56.8	426.9
Yugoslavia	78.5	46.1	29.9	103.7	44.6	0	94.3	8.9
Colombia	78.4	107.7	68.2	58.3	45.6	148.7	114.0	270.3
Brazil	77.9	266.5	10.4	52.2	87.5	679.9	49.1	0
Bangladesh	76.7	84.1	1.7	56.2	83.3	382.0	81.7	951.6
Oman	74.6	13.0	309.7	0	124.4	0	29.3	0
Iran	53.3	37.3	131.6	10.8	306.0	0	364.7	132.2
Sierra Leone	50.7	30.2	46.9	50.6	5.2	168.2	86.4	20.6
Bahrain	28.0	2.4	68.2	18.9	119.6	0	29.9	0
Kuwait	16.3	0	26.8	9.1	23.1	0	28.7	0

Source: Estimated by authors with data from *Government Finance Statistics* (1994) and *International Financial Statistics* (1994), as reported in Roy Bahl, Jorge Martinez-Vazquez, Michael Jordan, and Sally Wallace. 1993. "Intercountry Comparisons of Fiscal Performance." Technical Note No. 7. Guatemala Fiscal Administration Project, Atlanta: Georgia State University, College of Business Administration, Policy Research Center; Washington DC: KPMG Peat Marwick Policy Economics Group.

mala ranked 56th among the 66 countries, and exerted an effort that was only 79 percent of the international average. This analysis adds to our knowledge of Guatemala's low tax effort by showing that it was primarily due to a relatively low level of domestic income and sales taxation. Countries with Guatemala's economic and population structure typically raise about 14 percent of taxes from the individual income tax, whereas Guatemala raised only 3.4 percent. Taxes on the international trade sector, by contrast, were used more intensively in Guatemala than in other countries. This same conclusion holds if the comparison is made only with Latin American or Central American countries. For example, data for a more recent year show that there was not a major increase in reliance on the individual income tax, and Guatemala remained well below the Latin American average (Table 3.3).

Conclusions. From these analyses, one can conclude with some confidence that even when its particular economic characteristics and its tax structure are taken into account, Guatemala has been one of the lowest taxing countries in the world. It is not possible to repeat this exact analysis for the mid-1990s, because the necessary data for international comparisons are not available. However, comparison of raw tax-GDP ratios suggests that Guatemala's relative level of taxation has not risen since the late 1980s. The 1990 tax ratio of 6.93 percent was well below the average ratio for all countries, all Latin American countries, and all Central American countries in the sample. A comparison for a longer period for just the Central American countries shows that Guatemala (and El Salvador) were outliers with reductions in their tax ratio. During this period, every other Central American country showed an increase in the tax ratio.

Underlying the tax effort question is the issue of whether taxes are adequate to support the level of public expenditures that the nation wants or needs. The Guatemalan government faced a large budget deficit because it did not tax enough to support the services it provided, it overspent relative to the willingness of the population to provide tax support, or it was inefficient in delivering services per quetzal spent. The level of spending in Guatemala was not high relative to that in other countries with similar economic structures and levels of income, and the composition was different. An analysis of spending patterns for forty developing countries in the 1980s indicates that Guatemala spent an amount equivalent to 1.18 percent of GNP on education and 0.86 percent on health. The averages for all countries in the sample were 3.54 percent and 1.62 percent, respectively. For the eleven Latin American countries in the sample, the averages were 3.65 percent and 1.46 percent (Bahl, Jordan, Martinez-Vazquez, and Wallace, 1993). The IDB (1994) reported

TABLE 3.3 Distribution of Taxes in Guatemala and Latin America

	Latin American Countries[a]	Guatemala	
	1986-1987	1986-1987	1990
Personal Income Taxes	12.0%	4.6%	4.0%
Sales and Other Indirect Taxes	51.3	39.7	34.4
Property Taxes	3.6	1.7	2.5
Corporate Income Taxes	15.7	11.0	18.0
Export Taxes	3.8	15.1	3.3
Import Taxes	16.4	27.9	37.8
Total	100.0%	100.0%	100.0%

[a]Includes Argentina, Bolivia, Brazil, Chile, Colombia, Costa Rica, Ecuador, El Salvador, Mexico, Nicaragua, Panama, Paraguay, Peru, Uruguay and Venezuela.
Source: Roy Bahl, Jorge Martinez-Vazquez, Michael Jordan, and Sally Wallace. 1993. "Intercountry Comparisons of Fiscal Performance." Technical Note No. 7. Guatemala Fiscal Administration Project. Atlanta: Georgia State University, College of Business Administration, Policy Research Center; Washington, DC: KPMG Peat Marwick Policy Economics Group.

data that allow a comparison of spending in Guatemala and in other Latin American countries in 1993. Public expenditures as a percent of GDP was 10.6 percent of GDP in Guatemala in 1993, compared to an average of 22.6 percent for twenty four Latin American and Caribbean countries. For the other seven Central American nations, the average was 23.07 percent for 1993. There seems no escaping the fact that Guatemala is a low-spending country.

Coverage of the Tax Base

The average level of tax effort in Guatemala was low, but this does not mean that the effective tax rates levied on all families and all productive activities were low. In fact, certain economic sectors and households were taxed at a very low rate and others at a much higher rate under the previous tax structure. The reason for such differences in tax burden is that the tax base was narrowed by a combination of legal exemptions and deductions, incentives and preferential rate treatment, and by administrative shortcomings. This was a major problem with the pre-reform system.

In this section we present estimates of the "costs" of exemptions and deductions in terms of the higher nominal rates required to generate a given amount of revenue. This analysis points toward one avenue of reform: The level of revenues can be raised with lower nominal tax rates if tax bases are broadened.

Individual Income Tax

Only 3.9 percent of the economically active population was reached by the individual income tax in 1992, and only 4 percent of revenue was generated by this tax. This is surprising because about 14 percent of Guatemalan households had incomes above the national average level, and the top 10 percent of income earners accounted for half of all national income. Even by standards of tax practice in low-income countries, this was a thin coverage for the individual income tax. In Jamaica, for example, approximately 12 percent of the population was covered by the individual income tax in the late 1980s (Alm, Bahl, and Murray, 1991a).[6]

As may be seen in Table 3.4, the legal tax liability was equivalent to only 0.5 percent of total income earned, which is low by international standards. Even for those very high-income Guatemalans whose tax liability reached as high as 2 percent of income (the Q500,000 and over class), the rate was only about 2 percent.

One reason why the income tax base was so narrow was the high

TABLE 3.4 Distribution of Individual Income Tax Liability: 1992

Household Expanded Income Class (in thousands)	Number of Households	Expanded Income		Tax Liability		
		Amount (in billions)	Percentage of Total	Amount	Percentage of Total	Tax Liability as Percentage of Income
Q 0-18	1,283.7	Q9,223.9	21.6%	0.1	*	0
18-24	146.9	3,041.5	7.1	0.2	0.1%	0
24-36	156.9	4,614.4	10.8	0.9	0.4	0
36-60	115.5	5,265.8	12.3	3.0	1.3	0.1
60-90	47.5	3,435.3	8.0	3.9	1.7	0.1
90-125	21.7	2,259.7	5.3	11.7	5.1	0.5
125-250	31.1	5,178.0	12.1	41.0	17.7	0.8
250-500	11.0	3,800.8	8.9	52.3	22.6	1.4
500-over	5.5	5,915.9	13.8	117.8	51.0	2.0
Total	1,819.7	42,735.3	100.0	231.1	100.0	0.5

Note: Includes sole proprietorships and households that do not file tax returns. *Less than 0.1 percent.

Source: Ministry of Finance, Government of Guatemala, as reported to *Consultoria Para La Administracion Fiscal,* Policy Economics Group, KPMG Peat Marwick, and Policy Research Program, Georgia State University, 1991-1993.

level of personal exemptions and the liberal use of deductions.[7] The "average" head of household who filed an income tax return could reasonably claim deductions of Q18,800, equivalent to 220 percent of median household income. As the estimates[8] for 1992 (Table 3.5) indicate,

TABLE 3.5 Individual Income Tax Expenditures: 1992

	Individuals Affected		Tax Liability Impact		
	Number (thou- sands)	*Percent- age of Total*	*Amount (Q mill- ions)*	*Average per Affected Taxpayer*	*Percent- age of Total Current Tax Liability*
A. *Tax Expenditures Related to Personal Deductions*					
1. Personal Exemptions	350	13.0%	Q72	Q282	31.2%
2. Family Adjustment to Personal Exemption	54	2.0	10	174	4.3
3. Spouse Exemption	38	1.4	11	282	4.8
4. Dependent Exemption	66	2.5	36	552	15.6
B. *Other Tax Expenditures*					
1. Social Security Deduction	86	3.2%	Q10	Q113	4.3%
2. Insurance Premium Deduction	16	0.6	13	855	5.6
3. Professional Fee Deduction	14	0.5	4	268	1.7
4. Investment Incentive	*	§	1	8,604	0.4
5. Contribution to Education	*	§	†	‡	§
6. Other "Special Law" Deduction	*	§	5	18,780	2.2
7. Employment Incentive	*	§	†	‡	§
8. Reforestation Credit	*	§	2	45,912	0.9
9. Exempt Wage Bonus	149	5.5	36	241	15.6
10. Exempt Interest Income	61	2.3	147	2,421	63.6

*Less than Q1,000 taxpayers; †less than Q1,000,000 taxpayers; ‡less than Q100 taxpayers; §Less than .1 percent.

Source: Ministry of Finance, Government of Guatemala, as reported to *Consultoria Para La Administracion Fiscal*, Policy Economics Group, KPMG Peat Marwick, and Policy Research Program, Georgia State University, 1991-1993.

if the personal exemption had been eliminated, 350,000 households would have been affected (including those whose incomes were below the taxable floor but would have been liable for tax if the personal exemption were eliminated), and the revenue increase would have amounted to about 31 percent of estimated individual income tax collections in 1992.

The exclusion of certain types of income (e.g., certain types of interest income) from the individual income tax also contributed to the narrowness of the base. The full taxation of interest income would affect about 60,000 tax returns and, even with conservative assumptions about compliance, could increase the revenue yield of the individual income tax by more than 50 percent. Eliminating the exemptions for the wage bonus would increase revenues by about 15 percent.

Clearly, exemptions and deductions imposed a considerable revenue cost on the government of Guatemala. This cost was paid by other taxpayers in the form of higher rates. In 1989, the *average* individual income tax rate on taxable personal income was 2.1 percent for those who were in the system. If all deductions and all exemptions were eliminated, the average rate could have dropped to 0.65 percent and the same revenue would have been raised.

Company Income Tax

The major explanation for the narrow company income tax base in the pre-reform period was that several important components of income were excluded from taxation. The two most important exclusions were those business incomes that qualified for tax holidays, and the interest income from deposits with regulated financial institutions, marketed securities, and high-quality bonds. Moreover, many companies ended up paying little or no tax because some of the costs incurred in earning tax-exempt income were effectively deducted from other income earned in taxable activities. As there was no tax on dividends or on capital gains arising from the reinvestment of profits, owners of these companies were able to derive income that was taxed at neither the company nor the personal level.

Other features of the company tax also contributed to a narrowing of the base. The deductions of interest from the tax base were excessive during inflationary periods because part of the interest payments represented a compensation to lenders for the loss in the real value of loans. These interest payments did not represent a true cost to the firm. The rates used for depreciation of capital cost recovery also were too high for some assets. However, this effect on the tax base was mitigated by the negative impact of inflation on the value of deductions for depreciation over time. The deduction of investment expenditure in qualifying assets also narrowed the company tax base. Because of the narrow company tax base, the government relied on other measures to maintain revenues, such as a nonresident withholding tax of 34 percent.

Although the pre-reform company tax rate in Guatemala was not high by international standards, clearly tax rates could have been reduced significantly if measures were taken to broaden the company tax base. For example, if interest income had been taxable, it was estimated that for 1992 about 10,000 returns would have been affected (about 70 percent of all companies who should have filed). The revenue cost of the interest exemption was equivalent to about Q50 million, approximately 6 percent of 1992 collections (Table 3.6). The other important exclusions—from the standpoint of revenue costs—were the industrial decentralization credit and the preferential tax rates. Together, these two tax preferences implied an estimated revenue cost of more than Q87 million. Other tax preferences were not as costly. For example, over half of all firms took advantage of the bad debt deduction, but the revenue cost to the government was very small (less than Q3 million for 1992). In all, if every preferential treatment and exemption had been abolished, it was estimated that collections from the corporate income tax would have been 25 percent higher in 1992.

Value-Added Tax

The base of the value-added tax (VAT) was eroded in the pre-reform period by a combination of zero rating, exemptions, and evasion. Less than 35 percent of total domestic sales was reported as taxable under the VAT, and of this amount, only about 55 percent was taxed at the full 7 percent nominal rate. The result was that the effective tax rate was only 1.4 percent (Table 2.5). If all zero rating (except for exports) and exemptions were eliminated, the same revenues could have been raised with a statutory rate of 3.5 percent on consumption of domestically produced goods. A similar story may be told for imports (Table 2.6). The effective VAT rate on the value of imported goods was 5.3 percent, which was higher than that on domestic goods, but still well below the statutory 7 percent rate.

The joint revenue cost of legal exemptions, zero rating, and evasion was substantial. With full registration of all firms, and with neither zero rating (except for exports) nor exemptions, the value-added tax would have yielded Q1,138.1 million more revenue (229 percent) in 1988 than it did, or the 1988 revenues of Q496.6 million could have been raised with a rate of only 2.1 percent on total value-added. Birch and Due (1990, p.

TABLE 3.6 Business Income Tax Expenditures: 1992

Provision	Number of Firms	Percent of All Business Taxpayers	Tax Liability Impact Amount (Q millions)	Average Per Firm*
Agriculture:				
Rubber Promotion Credit	2	‡	§	0
Rabbit Promotion Credit	†	‡	§	N/A
Milk Promotion Incentive				
Credit	†	‡	§	N/A
Reforestation Credit	58	0.4%	Q4.6	Q 79,310
Export Promotion:				
Free Trade Zone Credit	9	0.1	1.5	16,667
Industrial Export Incentive				
Credit	460	2.8	10.4	22,609
Industry:				
Bad Debt Reserve Deduction	6,603	47.3	3.3	500
Investment Deduction	125	0.8	1.2	9,214
Employment Credit	†	‡	§	N/A
Industrial Decentralization				
Credit	132	0.8	43.0	325,758
Tourism Credit	33	0.2	1.6	48,485
Book Publishing Promotion				
Credit:	†	‡	§	N/A
Communication Credit	†	‡	§	N/A
Energy Credit	†	‡	5.0	N/A
Other:				
Education Incentive				
Deduction	†	‡	§	N/A
Tax Rates Below 34 Percent	8,204	58.7	44.4	5,406
Interest Income Exemption	9,710	69.5	51.0	5,249

*Financial institutions are not included; †Less than five firms; ‡Less than 0.05 percent of total; §Less that Q500,000.

Source: Ministry of Finance, as reported to *Consultoria Para La Administracion Fiscal*, Policy Economics Group, KPMG Peat Marwick, and Policy Research Program, Georgia State University, 1991-1993.

54) use a national income accounts approach to estimate that 1987 revenues from VAT could have been raised with a tax rate of between 3 and 5 percent.

While this thin coverage of the VAT in Guatemala was a serious problem, it was not all that unusual. Tanzi and Shome (1993, pp. 807-28) report a comparison for twenty-two developing and industrialized countries, showing revenues raised for each 1 percent of the VAT tax rate. The results indicate that the average amount of revenue raised per point of VAT was 0.37 percent of GDP. In Guatemala (1988 data) the revenue productivity per point of VAT was 0.34. Other Central American countries in the sample were Costa Rica (0.38) and Panama (0.22). Bird (1992, p. 122) reads the evidence as showing that general sales taxes in most developing countries derived half or more of their revenue from imports and probably did not reach more than 20 percent of domestic value added.

The Tax Structure and Interference with the Market

Certain features of the pre-reform tax system encouraged economic decisions that may not have promoted economic growth. For example, it encouraged companies to invest in structures and vehicles, when in the absence of tax preferences they might have chosen to invest in equipment or inventories; it biased their financing choice toward debt versus equity and led to thin capitalization of companies; and it channeled resources toward sectors with lower profitability. These hidden costs of distortionary taxes can be measured in terms of a less efficiently functioning economy.

In some cases (e.g., tax incentives) these distortions were introduced intentionally to remove some perceived bottleneck to economic growth. In others, the distortions were unintended side effects of structural changes introduced to reduce the tax burden or to solve an administrative problem. Either way, the size of these distortions appeared to be large and to impose a significant cost on Guatemalan society.

Interest and Inflation

In the pre-reform period, the structure of the Guatemalan company income tax introduced a major distortion in investment choices because of the tax treatment of interest income and expense, the differences between economic and book depreciation, and the preferential treatment of certain sectors of the economy under the tax-incentive programs. All of these biases are magnified at higher rates of inflation.

The biggest problem would appear to be the tax treatment of interest. In the pre-reform period, Guatemalan companies were able to borrow at negative real rates of interest (i.e., get paid to borrow funds), but they also were allowed a full deduction for interest paid. Allowing for the real *and* inflation component of interest costs as a deduction from taxable income, amounts to allowing the repayment of principal as a deduction.

One way to see the biases introduced by these features of the company tax is to calculate the marginal effective tax rates (METRs) on various kinds of investments, i.e., the percent by which the gross rate of return on an investment is reduced by taxes. A neutral tax system treats alternative investments evenhandedly and produces a uniform pattern of METRs across types of investment. Conversely, a non-neutral tax system causes a widespread dispersion in METRs for different sectors, types of assets, or sources of finance. As a diagnostic policy tool, the measurement of METRs is a powerful method for determining both the degree of neutrality contained in a current tax system and that which could be expected in alternative systems.

When this framework was applied to the pre-reform system of individual, corporate, and value-added taxation in Guatemala (Zodrow 1990), the following major results, summarized in Tables 3.7 and 3.8, were obtained:

- At zero inflation rates the tax system was roughly neutral in its treatment of investments in inventory, tools, office equipment, and furniture. However, because of the availability of partial expensing, investments in machinery, equipment, and vehicles were favored over other assets by the tax system.
- The dispersion in METRs across assets and sectors increased noticeably as the rate of overall price inflation rose.
- Debt finance was heavily favored over all forms of equity finance by the tax system. In fact, debt-financed investments tended to be subsidized by the tax system, resulting in revenue losses, an incentive for highly debt-laden financial structures on the part of companies, and a tendency toward an inefficient use of investment resources.
- The combination of partial expensing and interest deductibility on debt virtually guaranteed the presence of negative METRs on some assets.
- The impact of delayed refunds of value-added tax paid on purchases of capital goods raised METRs by 3 to 5 percentage points at a zero inflation rate and by 3 to 14 percentage points at a 30 percent rate of inflation.
- Inter-asset investment distortions appeared more significant than inter-sectoral distortions. Nonetheless, while the intersectoral variation in METRs was not large, it did increase noticeably at higher rates of inflation.

To move toward a more neutral tax system, it was necessary to address the asymmetry in the treatment of interest income and interest expenses, the differences between actual and allowed depreciation, and the differences in fiscal incentives offered to economic sectors and types of investments. The goal of a more neutral tax system also required that

TABLE 3.7 Marginal Effective Tax Rates: When Investments Are Financed With Retained Earnings, or New Equity Issues

	Rate of Inflation		
	0%	10%	30%
Asset			
Inventories	37.3%	37.3%	37.3%
Tools	30.4	51.6	81.0
Office Equipment and Furniture	38.9	61.4	83.0
Structures	29.2	38.2	43.4
Machinery, Equipment and Vehicles (with partial expensing)	10.4	26.0	45.3
Machinery, Equipment and Vehicles (without partial expensing)	24.4	39.0	56.9
Business Sector			
Agriculture, Forestry, Fishing	25.8	37.9	48.4
Mining	27.6	43.5	58.7
Manufacturing	26.5	39.0	49.8
Utilities	24.3	42.4	61.6
Construction	30.3	41.5	49.2
Commerce	28.4	40.5	50.2
Transportation/ Communication	27.9	39.8	49.3
Services	28.0	39.1	47.5

Source: George Zodrow. 1990. *Marginal Effective Tax Rates on Capital Income in Guatemala*. Technical Memorandum No. 13. Guatemalan Fiscal Administration Project. Atlanta: Georgia State University, College of Business Administration, Policy Research Center; Washington, DC: KPMG Peat Marwick Policy Economics Group.

the impact of inflation be controlled. But, before jumping immediately to the conclusion that full indexation of income taxes would solve many problems, the difficulties of dealing with inflation biases should be noted.

Introducing an adjustment mechanism for inflation—that is, some sort of indexation—carries with it a new set of costs. Besides the complex effects on expectations of private sector agents, the indexation of a tax system, especially of the company income tax, can present great administrative difficulties that would be better avoided. However, if an economy is experiencing an inflationary process, then the lack of an inflation adjustment mechanism leads to the series of distortions that have already been mentioned. The choice is a very difficult one. The only noncontroversial solution to the Guatemalan problem was to control inflation by controlling the government deficit and the money supply.

TABLE 3.8 Marginal Effective Tax Rates When Investments Are Financed With Debt

	Rate of Inflation		
	0%	10%	30%
Asset			
Inventories	0	-51.5%	-154.6%
Tools	-10.7%	-30.3	-88.8
Office Equipment and Furniture	2.6	-15.1	-85.5
Structures	-12.5	-50.4	-145.5
Machinery, Equipment and Vehicles (with partial expensing)	-41.8	-69.6	-143.4
Machinery, Equipment and Vehicles (without partial expensing)	-20.3	-49.6	-125.4
Business Sector			
Agriculture, Forestry, Fishing	-17.8	-51.0	-138.2
Mining	-15.0	-42.6	-122.8
Manufacturing	-16.8	-49.4	-136.1
Utilities	-20.2	-44.4	-118.3
Construction	-10.7	-45.4	-136.7
Commerce	-13.7	-47.0	-135.4
Transportation/ Communication	-14.6	-48.1	-136.6
Services	-14.3	-49.1	-139.3

Source: George Zodrow. 1990. *Marginal Effective Tax Rates on Capital Income in Guatemala*. Technical Memorandum No. 13. Guatemalan Fiscal Administration Project. Atlanta: Georgia State University, College of Business Administration, Policy Research Center; Washington, DC: KPMG Peat Marwick Policy Economics Group.

"Average-Marginal" Rates of Income Tax

The income tax rate schedule for both individuals and corporations was stated in terms of the average rate of tax for each rate bracket, not the marginal rate. As a result, a very high marginal rate was applicable to the first quetzal earned in each rate bracket.

Such a rate schedule is troublesome because it leads to tax avoidance behavior as taxpayers seek to avoid falling into a higher rate bracket. That is, substantial benefits could be had from successful maneuvers that would prevent a taxpayer from moving to the next higher rate bracket. This implied that many taxpayers could obtain a high pay-off from cheating, even if their average rate of tax was rather low, and that even taxpayers who were not near the top of a bracket may have planned their behavior on the assumption that they might be (Thuronyi 1990).

VAT Refunds and Credits

The government failed to pay refunds, and the tax structure did not allow credit for tax paid on capital purchases, or for "nondirect" inputs under the value-added tax. These features of the VAT, as practiced in Guatemala, created a bias against capital investments, seemed to undermine the public confidence in the tax, and appeared to lead to a greater amount of evasion via an overdeclaration of credits on inputs or an underdeclaration of receipts.

The refund problem was the most important. A firm is entitled to a refund when the input tax credit exceeds the tax due for the period. The policy of the Guatemalan government on the payment of these refunds has varied from time to time; but, in general, only limited amounts were paid. Because of the potentially drastic effects upon revenue and the belief that many of the claims were fraudulent, the government paid only relatively small amounts of the refunds due. The backlog of credits owed was reduced considerably by the issuance of 5-year bonds to firms in the late 1980s. However, there were at least Q45 million of claims outstanding in 1992 (though some private sector sources believed the true amount to be significantly higher). In practice, only refunds based on exports received audits to permit payment in bonds; refunds arising from other input tax credits continued outstanding.

The failure to pay refunds when a firm's input tax credit exceeds tax due on sales is destructive of morale and contrary to the basic nature of a value-added tax. The adverse effects are particularly severe on the export sector of the economy. Failure to provide the refunds increases the costs of goods exported, lessens the profits from exporting, and introduces a cascading element into the tax.

The VAT treatment of capital purchases also presented a problem, especially in a country that is committed to encouraging investment and capital formation. The practice of providing a credit for input tax on durable capital goods over a 5-year period (rather than expensing capital investments) introduced a bias against capital expenditures, an incentive for evasion, and administrative complications.

Tax Administration and Evasion

A major underlying problem with the Guatemalan tax system was poor administration and enforcement. Procedures were inadequate, recordkeeping and mechanization needed modernization, and staff in some departments were inadequately trained or too few in numbers. With regard to enforcement, for example, penalties for failure to file and pay VAT were relatively low and not effectively enforced, in part because of "discounting" and amnesties. The audit system was weak in its approach and understaffed to a point that many would-be evaders judged the probability of being detected as negligible.

The government's lack of legal authority to issue detailed regulations to fill in gaps in the statutes was an important obstacle to a smoothly functioning tax system. Tax statutes require such elaboration so that taxpayers (and tax collectors) can understand, the obligations to comply. Detailed regulations might have prohibited interpretations of the statutes that hindered tax collections (Thuronyi 1990).

The result of such difficulties with administration and enforcement was that the tax base was narrowed further still, revenues to support government services were lower than they otherwise would have been, and the system unfairly gave differential (arbitrary) treatment to individuals and businesses that were in essentially the same position (i.e., had the same income level, asset size, etc.). The tax structure was sometimes adjusted to accommodate weaknesses in the tax administration in ways that later appeared undesirable. For example, VAT credits on tax paid on inputs that were not directly a component of output were disallowed in order to protect against claims for personal expenditures as business deductions. The reason for not paying refunds on the value-added tax were also partly administrative, i.e., it is very difficult to monitor fraudulent claims. In some cases, administrative problems were made worse by provisions in the tax structure. Of 21,000 firms registered for the value-added tax, the smallest 13,749 contributed only Q7 million in revenues, i.e., only 3.6 percent of collections. If the VAT threshold had been increased to Q100,000 in sales, the tax administration task would have been reduced by 13,749 firms, but revenues would only have been reduced by Q7 million. This type of simplification in the tax structure not only would have reduced administrative costs, it would have freed up inspectors to spend more time working with the larger taxpayers. Overall, the administrative/compliance deficiencies were so great that the actual impact of the tax system on resource allocation and on the distribution of burdens was probably quite far from what was intended by the law.

One outgrowth of weak tax administration and lax enforcement is tax evasion—illegal noncompliance with the tax law. It is not easy to develop hard estimates of revenue loss due to evasion. This is because statistics are more readily available on those who do pay taxes than on those who do not. However, the data in Table 3.9 suggests the magnitude of evasion of the VAT in Guatemala in 1988. The total value of taxable purchases reported on the tax declarations in 1988 was Q7,333 million. However, the total value of taxable sales to registered businesses plus the total value of taxable imports reported by registered businesses was only

TABLE 3.9 Gap Between Reported Taxable Purchases and Reported Taxable Sales, 1988 (Millions of Quetzales)

A. Reported Taxable Purchases from Registered Businesses	Q7,333
B. Reported Taxable Sales to Registered Businesses and Taxable Imports of Registered Businesses	Q4,162
C. Gap between Taxable Purchases and Taxable Sales (A-B)	Q3,171
D. Gap as Percentage of Reported Taxable Purchases	56.8%

Source: Ministry of Finance, Government of Guatemala, as reported to *Consultoria Para La Administracion Fiscal*, Policy Economics Group, KPMG Peat Marwick, and Policy Research Program, Georgia State University, 1991-1993.

Q3,171 million. This is a gap of Q4,162 million between sales and purchases (or 56.8 percent of reported taxable purchases). Most of this gap can reasonably be attributed to evasion, either in the form of underreporting sales or overstating purchases.

An estimate of the gap between income tax potential and actual collections is provided in Table 3.10 for 1986. This calculation added legally exempt income to that reported on the income tax forms to obtain

TABLE 3.10 Estimate of Unreported Income: 1986 (Billions of Quetzales)

	Individuals	Businesses	Total
A. Income Reported on Tax Returns	Q2.2	Q0.4	Q1.8
B. Adjustments			
Income of legal non-filers	3.3	0.0	3.3
Legally excluded income[a]	0.7	0.3	1.0
Other allowable deductions[b]	1.1	1.1	2.2
Total adjustments	5.1	1.4	6.5
C. Adjusted reported income (A+B)	7.3	1.0	8.3
D. National income	9.0	7.0	16.0
E. Net income gap (C-D)[c]	1.6	6.1	7.7

[a]Includes tax-exempt interest, bonus income, income of tax-holiday businesses, and non-taxable supplements.

[b]Includes net operating loss carryovers, rental value of owner-occupied housing, and other special allowances.

[c]Detail may not correspond to the total because of rounding.

Source: Ministry of Finance, Government of Guatemala, as reported to *Consultoria Para La Administracion Fiscal*, Policy Economics Group, KPMG Peat Marwick, and Policy Research Program, Georgia State University, 1991-1993.

An estimate of the gap between income tax potential and actual collections is provided in Table 3.10 for 1986. This calculation added legally exempt income to that reported on the income tax forms to obtain a measure of "adjusted reported income." The difference between this and national income—about Q7.7 million or 48 percent of national income—represented a first estimate of what may be labelled the "net income gap." The implication of this calculation is that over half of potentially taxable income was not reported. This represents one estimate of the amount of income that was outside the tax system because of evasion.

Notes

1. See also Tait, Grätz and Eichengreen (1979) and Chelliah (1971).
2. This analysis is reported fully in Bahl, Martinez-Vazquez, Jordan, and Wallace (1993). The estimating equations for Table 3.1 are as follows:

Estimation Equations for Tax Effort

Estimates Based on 1984-1986 Data		
Lotz-Morss (1967):	$T/Y = 6.900 + 0.0015\,Y_p + 0.148\,XM_y$ $\qquad\quad (4.59)\quad (1.95)\qquad (5.39)$	$\bar{R}^2 = .61$
Bahl (1971):	$T/Y = 22.04 + 0.064\,N_y - 0.254\,A_y$ $\qquad\quad (10.01)\quad (-0.41)\quad (-3.83)$	$\bar{R}^2 = .37$
Chelliah, Bass and Kelly (1975):	$T/Y = 9.51 + 0.0020\,(Y_p\text{-}X_p) + 0.187\,N_y + 0.230X'_y$ $\qquad\quad (5.66)\quad (1.90)\qquad\qquad (1.25)\qquad (3.31)$	$\bar{R}^2 = .43$

where T/Y = the ratio of taxes (excluding social security contributions) to GDP,
Y_p = per capita Gross National Product in U.S. dollars, and
XM_y = the ratio of the sum of the values of commodity exports plus commodity imports to GDP,
$(Y_p\text{-}X_p)$ = per capita non-export income in U.S. dollars,
N_y = the percentage share of mining (including petroleum) in GDP,
X'_y = the ratio of non-mineral exports to GNP, and
A_y = the percentage share of agriculture in GDP.

Source: Estimated by authors with data from *Government Finance Statistics* (1994) and *International Financial Statistics* (1994), as reported in Roy Bahl, Jorge Martinez-Vazquez, Michael Jordan, and Sally Wallace. 1993. "Intercountry Comparisons of Fiscal Performance." Technical Note No. 7. Guatemala Fiscal Administration Project. Atlanta: Georgia State University, College of Business Administration, Policy Research Center; Washington, DC: KPMG Peat Marwick Policy Economics Group.

3. This method was originally developed and applied to states in the United States by the U.S. Advisory Commission on Intergovernmental Relations (1991).

4. As reported in the International Monetary Fund, *Government Finance Statistics* (1994).

5. The regression coefficient shows the marginal responsiveness of revenues (in percent terms) to differences in the tax base (in percent terms), after controlling for the level of per capita income. The predicted value from the equation can be converted to an estimate of the amount of tax expected if a country performs at the regression average.

6. By standards of practice in other countries, 3.9 percent may not be so surprising a number. Goode (1984, p. 102-103) points out that as recently as 1939, the U.S. individual income tax covered only 5 percent of the population. Since that time, the U.S. coverage has risen to over 90 percent. The U.S. figure for the income tax revenue share in 1939 was 18 percent.

7. The impacts of the number of deductions, personal exemptions, and income exemptions are summarized in Martinez-Vazquez (February 1989).

8. "Estimates" in this case means estimates of what the pre-reform system would have yielded if no changes had been enacted.

4

Objectives and Approach

There are many ways to "fix" an inadequate tax system, and the Guatemalan government faced many choices and tradeoffs. A good reform should be well thought out and will be based on a government's priorities among economic efficiency, vertical equity, fairness, revenue targets, and tax administration.[1] Guatemala's structural reform was well thought-out, reflected a set of priorities that squared with the economic policies of the government, and generally followed the rules of good tax practice.

Structural Goals

The first objective of the tax reform was to restore public confidence in the tax system. There had long been a serious tax compliance problem in Guatemala, and by 1991 it appeared to be getting worse. This compliance problem contributed substantially to the lack of public confidence in the tax system. To regain that confidence, the tax reform would have to:

- *improve the fairness of the system.* Those with similar incomes or in similar business situations should be treated the same under the tax system. As long as the public believes that there are some who receive preferential treatment under the law or the system of enforcement, they will resist compliance.
- *rationalize the tax structure.* The public will not have confidence in a system that does not seem "reasonable." In the Guatemalan case, a personal income tax with marginal effective rates of over 1,000 percent, a value-added tax that did not provide refunds

due, or a company income tax that placed high tax rates on equity finance and long-lived investments but low tax rates on debt finance, all seemed unreasonable.

- *simplify the tax structure.* Complexity and/or lack of instructions also raises problems with public confidence. The public will not have confidence in a tax system that it does not understand, and tax administration becomes more difficult and costly. Special treatments (loopholes) were a major source of unfairness and complexity in the Guatemalan system.

- *reduce compliance costs.* The resistance to paying taxes multiplies if taxpayers are asked to incur a large cost in the process of tax payment. Compliance procedures needed to be streamlined, an ample supply of forms and clear instructions had to be available, so that each taxpayer would be certain of his or her rights and responsibilities.

- *remove the arbitrariness from the administrative system.* The Guatemalan public had no confidence in a system that they believed to be administered in an ad hoc fashion, e.g., taxes were collected only where they were easy to collect (withholding). The public had no confidence either in an ineffective administration that allowed widespread overstatement of input taxes on the value-added tax or corruption in the payment of import duties. The tax administration needed to be more professional. This could be accomplished by developing a master file, installing an effective system of presumptive assessment, computerizing recordkeeping, streamlining the audit process, and training tax administrators to do the job of assessment and collection.

- *toughen the enforcement of the tax system.* The Guatemalan public did not believe in a tax system that a government was unwilling to enforce. In 1991, the public had every right to believe that if they did not fully pay taxes in a timely manner there was a low probability that they would be detected, and even if they were caught, the penalty rate would not be severe. Frequent tax amnesties, inadequate audit procedures, and long overdue tax delinquencies were all symptoms of a poorly enforced system in which the public did not have confidence.

- *give the public some confidence that the government is spending the tax money well.* One route to this is more effective budgeting and program evaluation, but another is macroeconomic fiscal responsibility. The presence in Guatemala of large and growing deficits and increased reliance on domestic and foreign borrowing were not conducive to building confidence.

The second objective was to develop a tax structure that was consistent with the government's economic policies. At the time the reform program was structured in 1990-91, there were three broad areas of economic policy with which the tax structure reform had to be consistent: The first was a return to steady economic growth with stable prices. This suggests that a primary concern of the new tax program would be to bring the deficit under control. One way to do this was with increased revenue mobilization, either through tax increases, tougher enforcement, or more reliance on user and benefit charges. Elimination of the deficit required a tax increase equivalent to about 2.6 percent of GDP at 1990 levels. This required a tax-GDP ratio of 9.5 percent (versus the existing 6.9 percent) in that year.

The second principle was promotion of export growth. The basic tax structure was in place to provide this support, since nontraditional exports were zero-rated under the value-added tax. What remained in 1992 was to extend zero-rating to all exports and to remove some irritants, such as the slow crediting of certain input purchases.

Finally, an important element of Guatemalan economic growth was the attraction of foreign capital. It was not likely in 1992 that tax incentives were the right instrument to attract foreign capital, since Guatemala was already one of the lowest-taxing countries in the region. A stable fiscal situation and better infrastructure and services were the better route to increasing the comfort level of foreign investors.

Basic to all of this was the question of the right strategy for formulating the tax rates and tax bases under the new system. One approach was to "pick winners," as in the pre-reform system, i.e., to give preferential treatment to certain firms and to impose a commensurately higher rate on others. The other was to establish a broad-based tax system, with the lowest tax rate possible given the revenue constraint. The Guatemalan Fiscal Project took the position that the government desired to increase the tax share of GDP, to restructure the system to enhance the competitive position of domestic producers and exporters, and to attract new capital. Consistent with this strategy was a tax system with the lowest possible tax rates.

The third objective of the reform was to establish an appropriate pattern of vertical equity, i.e., the proper distribution of tax burdens among the rich, the middle class, and the poor. If the pre-reform tax system reflected the desires of the government in this regard, a proportional to mildly progressive system could be taken as the objective. The equity goals suggested for this reform were (1) minimize the amount of tax the low income households must pay, (2) do not worsen the overall progressivity of the system, and (3) increase the number of high-income people involved in the payment of taxes. At the outset, the Project rejected the idea that the tax system might be reformed to fine-tune the distribution of income. For one thing, the level of taxes in Guatemala was so low that any feasible reform could not have had much of an impact. A second issue was administration. Discretionary changes that taxed the rich heavily probably could not be fully enforced, and the potential distributional gains might be lost to evasion. Third, the pre-reform tax system did not reach the very poor to any great extent. The VAT did not cover basic foodstuffs, and most taxes were collected in Guatemala City. Finally, the whole idea of this reform was to strengthen the Guatemalan economy by raising revenues in a more neutral way, through broad tax bases and low tax rates. An interventionist approach, led by vertical equity concerns, would have been out of step with this objective.

A fourth objective was to improve the horizontal equity of the Guatemalan tax system. That is, the base of the income taxes and the VAT need to be broadened to include most sources of income and most objects of consumption. In this way, all individuals and businesses would face a similar tax burden, and economic choices would be driven more by the market and less by the tax structure. The broader the tax base, the lower would be the tax rates.

The Project began its work with a specific revenue neutrality constraint. The goal was to design a structurally superior system that would produce about the same revenue as the system in force. While it was acknowledged that changes in the tax structure would change the elasticity, and that therefore one-period revenue neutrality was about all one could hope for, the work did not begin with a goal of raising taxes. But, as in many countries that start out with the more noble goal of structural reform, the Guatemalan Fiscal Project eventually turned to revenue mobilization.[2]

Reform Strategy

How does a country restructure its tax system to move toward these objectives? There are divided opinions on the best approach—Should reform be piecemeal and incremental or should the system will be "shocked" with a comprehensive reform?[3] If there is a conventional wisdom, it is that incremental reforms have the best chance for success. The arguments in favor of this approach are powerful. The public and the government are accustomed to the present system; marginal changes are likely to be understood and therefore accepted; the typical less developed country (LDC) tax administration system is not equipped to absorb big changes.

The other choice is comprehensive reform. There are strong arguments for shocking the whole system. First, the existing system may have gotten so out of sync with what the government wants to achieve with tax policy that no amount of incremental reform can repair things. Second, the best chance to gain acceptance of the painful parts of a tax reform is to implement them simultaneously with measures that provide taxpayer relief. Third, if the primary objective of the system is to put to right some important distortions in relative prices, then large changes are almost certainly called for. Tax-price elasticities of saving, investment, work effort, evasion, and so forth, are low; therefore, the rate changes necessary to cause a reallocation of resources must be large.[4] Finally, comprehensive reform tends to be associated with a particular political administration, and there is need to "get on with it" while the power is in place and while there is still enthusiasm for the reform program.

The Guatemalan tax reform was in the comprehensive reform tradition. The approach was to ask what is wrong with the present tax system—How is it at odds with what the government would like to achieve? Does it square with modern thinking about the elements of a "good" tax structure? and What changes should be made to the Guatemalan tax system to bring it more in step with the objectives of government policy? The scope of the reform is the entire tax system, and the tax administration, with the goal of introducing consistent changes in all major taxes.

In early 1992, the Project and the government formulated a fiscal reform program that was intended to achieve many of the objectives just described. Congress accepted most of the proposals and enacted a major reform that became effective in mid-1992 (fiscal year 1993). Most of the proposals to change the tax structure were in the direction of broadening the tax base, simplifying the system, removing tax features that led to market distortions, and minimizing the impact on low-income Guatemalans. The proposals are evaluated in the next three chapters in five respects:

1. The revenue impact.
2. The revenue-income elasticity.
3. The distribution of tax burdens.
4. Possible allocative effects.
5. Tax administration and compliance costs.

Notes

1. Not everyone agrees with this approach. There are various opinions about the proper objectives of tax reform in developing countries. Some would argue

that administration is so deficient that the only reasonable goal to set is the raising of revenue. Others would begin with political feasibility and discard all reform options that did not meet that test. A good review of the issues is presented in Tanzi (1991, pp. 157-74).

2. Gillis (1989, pp. 236-237) notes that in the highly successful Indonesian reform of the mid-1980s, the program turned from revenue neutrality to revenue enhancement after the work had begun.

3. This section draws on Bahl's (1991a, p. 28) discussion of the Jamaican tax reform. A very thoughtful review of the points raised here is in Goode (1993).

4. The evidence on these price elasticities is reviewed in Gandhi (1987).

5

Individual Income Tax: Proposals and Reforms

The individual income tax has not been heavily used in Guatemala.[1] In 1990, it accounted for only 0.4 percent of GDP. Moreover, revenues from the individual income tax had slipped as a share of GDP from 0.44 percent in 1987. Before the revenue potential of the individual income tax could be realized, significant structural reform would be required. In this chapter, we evaluate the pre-reform system, lay out the recommendations of the Guatemalan Fiscal Project and the reform program adopted by the government, and project the impact of the reforms.

The Pre-reform System

The tax was beset by a number of structural problems before the reform. These problems resulted in a relatively unfair distribution of tax burdens and altered taxpayer work and investment behavior, thus decreasing the economic efficiency of the tax system and complicating administration and tax compliance. Taxable income was far removed from a comprehensive base, thus encouraging the government to make up revenue through higher tax rates (Break 1991). The number and level of exemptions resulted in a relatively large revenue cost to the government. There were, in addition, problems with the administration of the tax that called for changes in the statutes, the procedures, and the staffing. The proposed reform program addressed the structural problems and laid the groundwork for a more efficient administration.[2]

The Tax Base

The pre-reform individual income tax system was hampered by a narrow tax base. While this system imposed a tax on both residents and nonresidents, it only taxed Guatemalan-source income. Taxpayers were not required to report foreign-source income. For Guatemalan residents, the main importance of these rules was that income from investments abroad was legally exempt from tax in Guatemala. Because such income is often exempt in the source country, a zero rate of tax could be legally achieved by Guatemalan residents by investing abroad.

Nonresident individuals (those present in the country for six months or less) were subject to a withholding tax at a 34 percent rate under the pre-reform system, with preferential, reduced rates of 12.5 percent for dividends and of 25 percent for interest. With respect to payments for services performed by nonresidents, the general rule was that the income was Guatemalan-source if the services were performed in Guatemala. Payments for technical services provided to government entities where the technical assistance was paid from abroad were exempt from tax. When the individual performing the services was a resident of a country with territorial taxation, the effect of this provision was to exempt the income from taxation. This benefited the individual taxpayer. In the case of a citizen of a country with worldwide taxation and a foreign tax credit (such as the United States), the exemption generally redounded to the benefit of the treasury of the country in which the individual paid income tax.[3]

Tax Rates

The pre-reform rate schedule (fixed in October 1987) was progressive, with rates from 4 percent (for the first Q5,000) increasing to 34 percent for incomes in over Q130,000. The individual income tax code did not provide for any indexation of brackets, exemptions, deductions, or other tax relief. The progressive rate schedule of the tax code provided a lucrative loophole for high-income taxpayers. Since separate filing by family members was allowed, a high-income family member could shift income to lower-income family members and thereby reduce the overall family tax liability. (The same could be done for capital income, but since capital income is largely exempt, the benefits of shifting were relatively small.)

The rate schedule for individuals (as well as for corporations) was stated in terms of the *average* rate of tax for each rate bracket, *not* the marginal rate. This means that once a taxpayer's income moved to the next higher bracket, the higher tax rate was applied to each quetzal, not just to the marginal income. The resulting marginal rate schedule was a discontinuous one, with the marginal rate of tax generally corresponding to the average rates set forth in the schedule but with a very high marginal rate applicable to the first quetzal earned in each rate bracket

(Thuronyi 1990). For example, an individual with Q30,000 of income would pay a 12 percent rate (Q3,600). The next tax rate of 14 percent would apply to *all* income, so that if the individual's income increased by one quetzal, the tax would increase by Q600; the marginal rate on that quetzal would therefore be 60,000 percent. The statutory average and effective marginal rate schedules of this income tax structure are compared in Table 5.1.

This situation was inappropriate, and led to tax avoidance behavior as taxpayers sought to avoid falling into a higher rate bracket. Experience shows that the revenue loss due to underreporting can be quite substantial. Clotfelter (1983) found that the elasticity of underreported income with respect to the marginal tax rate was 0.84 in the United States. In other words, a 10 percent increase in the marginal tax rate would lead to

TABLE 5.1: Statutory Average and Effective Marginal Rates for Individuals: Pre-reform

Taxable Income (Quetzales)	Average Tax Rate[a] (in percent)	Effective Marginal Tax Rate on 1 Quetzal (in percent)
Q0 - 5,000	4%	---
5,000.01 - 10,000	6	10,000%
10,000.01 - 15,000	8	20,000
15,000.01 - 20,000	10	30,000
20,000.01 - 30,000	12	40,000
30,000.01 - 40,000	14	60,000
40,000.01 - 50,000	16	80,000
50,000.01 - 60,000	18	100,000
60,000.01 - 70,000	20	120,000
70,000.01 - 80,000	22	140,000
80,000.01 - 90,000	24	160,000
90,000.01 - 100,000	26	180,000
100,000.01 - 110,000	28	200,000
110,000.01 - 120,000	30	220,000
120,000.01 - 130,000	32	240,000
In excess of 130,000	34	260,000

[a]The average tax rate applies to *all* income of an individual in a given taxable income bracket. For example, an individual with taxable income of Q25,000 pays 12 percent of Q25,000 or Q3,000.

Source: Victor Thuronyi. 1990. *Company and Individual Income Taxation: Structure and Administration*. Technical Memorandum No. 10. Guatemala Fiscal Administration Project. Atlanta: Georgia State University. Policy Research Center; Washington, D.C.: KPMG Peat Marwick Policy Economics Group; and computations by authors.

a reduction in reported income of over 8 percent. Given Guatemala's excessively high marginal tax rates and relatively weak administration, tax evasion was likely to be widespread.

Given the complexities of the pre-reform rate schedule, it was an obvious candidate for conversion to a conventional marginal tax rate schedule or to a flat-rate tax schedule.[4] In addition to eliminating the notch problem by changing the rate structure from average to marginal rates, simplification would also be served by reducing the number of brackets. The large number of rate brackets may have made sense under the pre-reform rate schedule. As pointed out in Thuronyi (1990), the fact that the rates increased by only 2 percentage points discontinuously avoided the even higher marginal rates at the beginning of each bracket that would have resulted from large jumps in an average rate schedule. A conventional marginal rate schedule would smooth the impact of moving from one bracket to the next and would therefore naturally reduce the number of brackets that were needed to avoid severe notches.

Deductions

The pre-reform system allowed a relatively expansive array of deductions.[5] While some of the deductions had merit on an equity basis, many simply overly complicated the system and narrowed the tax base. Each taxpayer was allowed a personal exemption of Q5,000 (Q6,500 if the taxpayer had dependents), and an additional deduction of Q2,000 (Q3,000 for taxpayers whose sole income was from employment). While there was no good economic reason for the additional separate deduction, it appeared to be a holdover from earlier systems. This deduction could easily be merged with the personal exemption to form a new type of basic deduction.

The deductions for dependents were Q2,500 for the taxpayer's spouse, Q1,800 for each child under age 21 or unable to work, and Q1,800 for other qualified dependents of the taxpayer. These combined personal exemptions could add up to Q16,400 or more for an average family. However, single individuals with no dependents were allowed total personal exemptions of Q7,000-Q8,000.

The differential exemptions, based on marital status and family size, called into question the horizontal equity of the system. Horizontal equity refers to the "equal" tax treatment of individuals in "similar situations" and is generally regarded as a basic tenet of good tax policy (Musgrave and Musgrave 1984). Exemptions for dependents may be one way to equalize the situations of taxpayers with similar incomes but differences in family size. However, the level of the deduction may be viewed as providing a relatively generous fiscal benefit to families at the expense of single taxpayers.

A deduction for up to Q3,000 was allowed for services performed by a professional certified by a university, e.g., lawyers, public accountants, civil engineers, doctors, dentists, and others. One motivation for this deduction was to provide a means of auditing professionals. As reported by Thuronyi (1990), there were many reasons that the deduction did not seem to serve this purpose. First, many individual (professional) taxpayers did not need to submit receipts to the tax authorities because they did not file returns. Second, processing the receipts required drawing administrative resources from other, perhaps more revenue-productive, uses. Third, since only a small percentage of the population paid income tax, even if professionals issued receipts to these persons and reported the income represented by those receipts, they could still fail to report income for services rendered to nontaxpayers. Additionally, taxpayers with expenses over the Q3,000 limit would not require a receipt. Another reported justification for the deduction for professional services was to improve the competitive position of professionals vis-à-vis persons who were not certified. For example, the provision might encourage individual taxpayers to hire a certified public accountant as opposed to a bookkeeper who is not a CPA. Although it is understandable that professionals might have an interest in preserving this deduction, and their opposition to its elimination might present a political obstacle, the deduction does not have a solid tax policy justification. Moreover, the provision imposed a recordkeeping burden on taxpayers and complicated both the tax form and tax administration. It did not make sense to devote scarce audit resources to this item, given all the other problems of noncompliance with which auditors must deal (Thuronyi, p. 26).

The Q3,000 deduction for professional services could be eliminated by outright repeal or by combining it with the personal exemption. In either case, the revenue effects would be relatively small because the average amount deducted for professional services was approximately Q940 in 1989.

Individuals could also deduct premiums for term life insurance, which is another violation of the principle of horizontal equity. Life insurance proceeds received by reason of the death of the insured were also exempt from income tax, making life insurance a highly preferred investment. The presence of a deduction for premiums also adds additional complexity to the overall income tax structure. This deduction reduces the progressivity of the income tax structure since wealthier taxpayers are more likely to purchase insurance. Therefore, the deduction was used disproportionately by high-income individuals. There is little sound reason to use the tax code to encourage such investment.

Individuals were also allowed to deduct social security contributions (IGSS) and contributions to retirement plans. However, pensions and social security benefits received were not taxable under the pre-reform system. This combination of deductibility for contributions and exemption for pension and social security receipts encouraged investment in retirement savings and may also have encouraged early retirement. The evidence of the influence of preferential treatment for retirement savings in developing countries is virtually nonexistent. In developed countries, a number of empirical studies have been undertaken to determine the elasticity of savings (retirement and other) to after-tax rates of return. The results have been mixed. Savings appear to be responsive to changes in the after-tax rate of return (Boskin 1978), but the magnitude may not be very large (Bovenberg 1989). With respect to targeted savings vehicles (such as retirement savings), the empirical evidence is mixed: some analyses suggest that preferential tax treatment may only nominally stimulate total saving (Gale and Scholz 1993), but others have found stronger responses (Venti and Wise 1987). Therefore, the preferential treatment of retirement savings in the tax code may complicate the system, while having relatively little impact on actual saving. In fact, the tax expenditure associated with the preferential treatment may be larger than the increase in private savings. The government itself could eliminate the preference and establish a more lucrative public pension pool.

Charitable contributions made by a business were deductible, but contributions made by individuals who did not conduct a business were not deductible. This resulted in more complexities as individuals sought to shelter income through such contributions.

To summarize the effect of personal deductions, consider the following two cases. Case one is an employed married individual who purchased life insurance for Q400, who incurred Q1,000 for expenses for professional services, whose spouse does not work outside the household, and who has three children (our data indicate that three is an average number of dependents). Case two is an employed single individual who did not purchase life insurance but did incur Q500 for professional services and has no dependents. The deductions allowed for each are shown in Table 5.2.

An individual with an average-sized family could have earned up to Q17,800 without incurring any income tax liability, while a single individual could have earned less than one-half that amount and still be outside the tax net. However, since these amounts were large enough to render the vast majority of employees exempt from income tax, the

TABLE 5.2: Deductions For Two Hypothetical Taxpayers

Exemptions and Deductions	Case 1	Case 2
Personal exemption	Q6,500	Q5,000
Spousal exemption	2,500	0
Children	5,400	0
Professional services	1,000	500
Additional deduction	2,000	2,000
Life insurance	400	0
Total	Q17,800	Q7,500

inequities associated with differential deductions and the complex rate structure were not a serious issue for low-income individuals. The relatively high tax threshold resulted in making less than 1 percent of the population liable for any amount of income tax.

Fringe Benefits

In addition to personal exemptions and deductions, various forms of income from labor were exempt from tax. The most important was the exemption of *aguinaldos* (Christmas bonuses) in amounts up to 200 percent of monthly salary (Thuronyi 1990, p. 30). These types of deductions are not unusual, especially in income tax structures in developing countries (Alm, Bahl, and Murray 1991a). *Aguinaldos* exclusions are inequitable in that employees of one company may receive preferential treatment compared with employees of another company. (Most employers pay an *aguinaldo* of 100 percent, but some pay 200 percent, and the self-employed are treated differently). The other problem with allowing the tax-deductible bonus is that it narrows the income tax base, and forces the government to levy a higher rate in order to meet its revenue objectives.[6]

Interest Income

Most interest income was exempt from individual income tax. This exemption is a major tax expenditure and a major source of unfairness in the distribution of tax burdens. As may be seen in Table 3.5, the exemption of interest income had an estimated revenue cost equivalent to nearly 64 percent of collections. The *average* amount claimed is more than Q2,400. If interest income were fully taxed under the present system, the average individual income tax rate could be reduced by more than half, and the same revenue could be raised. This assumes, of course, that there would be no capital flight, displacement of eligible interest bearing deposits, or reduction in the compliance rate. In all likelihood, there would be some behavioral adjustments associated with higher taxation of capital income (Bird 1992). Also pointed out by McLure, et al. (1989), the abolition of a weak system of taxation of interest income could actually increase revenue.

The exemption of interest income also compromises the vertical and horizontal equity of the individual income tax. Since interest income accrues primarily to higher income families, its exemption redistributes the tax burden from higher bracket to lower bracket taxpayers. It also discriminates in favor of those in any given income bracket who earn more of their income from interest and against those who earn more from wages.

Proposed and Actual Reforms

The Project proposed that the system of average-marginal rates be changed to a more conventional marginal rate schedule. This change would remove the notch problem that characterized the pre-reform system. The Project also proposed that the government consider adopting either a flat-rate tax or a progressive-rate schedule with fewer brackets.

Flat Tax

A flat-rate tax has much appeal. It is simple and understandable. If introduced together with a standard deduction that is indexed, it totally eliminates any inflation tax. If deductions are not indexed, those in the tax system will not be bumped to a higher tax rate bracket even though their real income has not increased. A flat rate also gets around the administrative problems that arise when capital income is withheld at a single rate and must be grossed up to "fit" a higher individual tax rate. The flat-rate tax has been successfully implemented in a number of countries, including Jamaica, Hong Kong, and Bolivia (Bird and Oldman 1990), and has been discussed as an option for other countries, including the United States.[7]

The flat-rate tax proposal was rejected by the Guatemalan government, mostly because it would have been too big a shock to the system. Also, with VAT increases and company tax reductions under consideration, abandoning the progressive income tax rate structure would have made the reform seem too "pro-rich." This is somewhat akin to the situation described in Bird and Oldman (1990).

TABLE 5.3: Individual Income Tax Structure Under the 1992 Reform

Taxable Income	Marginal Tax Rate	Tax Liability
Less than Q20,000	0.15	0.15 × (taxable income)
Q20,000-Q65,000	0.20	Q3,000 + 0.20 × (taxable income - Q20,000)
Greater than Q65,000	0.25	Q12,000 + 0.25 × (taxable income - Q65,000)

Progressive Rate

The alternative recommendation was a progressive rate schedule (but with a significant reduction in the number of rate brackets). This, Guatemalan officials felt, would provide less of a shock to the taxpaying population, would have more political appeal than the flat-rate tax alternative, and would move to simplify the system. There are drawbacks to the progressive rate structure. It leaves open the possibility of "bracket creep," and the degree of graduation here suggests a substantial incentive to avoid being bumped to a higher rate bracket. As discussed earlier, successively higher tax rates increase the incentive for tax evasion. There is a tendency in many countries for the elasticity and equity "benefits" of progressive rate taxes to be compromised by providing loopholes to offset the potentially greater tax burdens on higher income taxpayers. Another disadvantage of the progressive rate schedule is that it complicates the possibility of a withholding tax on interest income.

The Guatemalan government decided to adopt a progressive, conventional marginal rate schedule structured as shown in Table 5-3. The new rate schedule would reduce total income tax revenue, since it reduced the number of brackets, dropped the top rate, and eliminated the average-marginal rate practice. The revenue loss in 1993 for this change alone was estimated at 12 percent of what the previous system would have yielded (see Tables 5.4 and 5.5).[8]

Standard Deductions

The Project recommended that the system of deductions be replaced with a standard deduction of Q20,000, and that the indexation of the standard deduction for inflation be considered. The complicated pre-reform system of deductions was not being monitored effectively by the tax administration system, with the result that it was not clear that the

TABLE 5.4: Individual Income Tax Reforms: Revenue Implications

	Revenue Effect (FY94)	
	Amount (in Millions of Quetzales)	Percentage of Baseline Revenue
Tax Interest Income at 10% Percent	Q71	17.2%
Replace Itemized Deduction With a Combined Q24,000 Standard and Social Security Deduction	-74	-18.0
20% Deduction for Reinvestment of Profits	-21	-5.1
Tax Capital Gains at 15% Separate Rate	8	1.9
Change to New Marginal Rate Schedule	-43	-10.4
Allow Credit for VAT Paid	-167	-40.5
Gross Sales Tax Estimated Payments (1.5%)	12	2.9
Total	Q -226	-54.9%

distributional objectives of the deductions were being achieved. More-over, inflation had so eroded the value of the deductions that they could not have a major effect on economic decisions or provide any significant measure of subsidy to those in need. If the system had been properly policed, it would have led to substantial increases in administrative and compliance costs (employers were responsible for much of the validation of the deductions claimed).[9]

An advantage of the standard deduction versus the special-purpose deductions is vertical equity. If certain deductions are claimed by high-income taxpayers, e.g., the professional fee deduction, then the pre-reform system is less progressive than would be a system that allows all taxpayers to claim the same quetzal amount. However, under a progres-sive rate, the value of the deduction is greater for high-income than for low-income individuals.

The government finally adopted a standard deduction, and set the amount at Q24,000. No provision was made for indexing. This change would have resulted in an estimated revenue loss equivalent to about one-fifth of estimated collections in 1994 if the pre-reform system had not been changed. However, these revenue losses are probably overstated because, with inflation, there would have been substantial pressure on the Guatemalan government to increase the level of deductions under the pre-reform system.

TABLE 5.5: Individual Income Tax Policy Reform: Estimated Impacts

1. Revenue Impact:

	Fiscal Years (in Q millions)		
	1992	1993	1994
Baseline Projection	Q243	Q314	Q412
Tax Modernization Program	284	166	198
Difference	41	-148	-214
Tax Liability GDP Elasticity			
Baseline Projection	NA	1.99	2.25
Tax Modernization Program	NA	1.54	1.61

2. Tax Burden Impact (1992):

Household Income Class	Baseline Number of Households (in thousands)	Baseline Effective Tax Rate	Tax Modernization Program Effective Tax Rate	Tax Modernization Program Difference in Effective Tax Rate
Under Q2,465	180.9	0	0	0
Q2,465 to 3,750	182.2	0	0	0
Q3,750 to 5,250	181.5	0	0	0
Q5,250 to 7,250	182.4	0	0	0
Q7,250 to 9,450	181.3	0	0	0
Q9,450 to 12,700	182.9	0	0	0
Q12,700 to 17,600	182.4	0	0	0
Q17,600 to 25,550	181.3	0	0	0
Q25,550 to 43,250	181.5	0	0	0
Q43,250 and over (total)	183.4	1.0%	0.5%	-0.5%
Q43,250 to 74,450	93.3	0.1	0	-0.1
Q74,450 to 230,000	71.6	0.6	0.2	-0.4
Over Q230,000	18.5	1.7	1.0	-0.7
Total	1,819.7	0.5%	0.3%	-0.2%

3. Number of Tax Units in 1992:

(a) With increased liability	6,829
(b) With reduced liability	80,053
(c) Made taxable	4,625
(d) Made nontaxable	65,414

Source: Ministry of Finance, Government of Guatemala, as reported to *Consultoria Para La Administracion Fiscal*, Washington D.C.: Policy Economics Group: KPMG Peat Marwick; Atlanta: Georgia State University, Policy Research Center.

Additional Deductions

The government decided to allow four additional deductions: social security payments (taken as part of the withholdings scheme); child support; medical expenses; and a VAT credit equivalent to 7 percent of income. The first three of these deductions are allowed for social purposes. The fourth is meant to provide an incentive for increased efficiency in the collection of the value-added tax and to offset some of the regressivity of the tax. The reasoning is that consumers will demand receipts if they must have them to claim an income tax credit. If sellers issue receipts, audit will be an easier task, although it may encourage evasion through the production of false receipts.[10]

The VAT credit is given by employers as part of withholding: 50 percent is part of regular pay period deductions and the remaining 50 percent is given at the end of the year. In practice, employees do not have to prove their payment of VAT in order to receive the credit, hence the collection efficiency objective of this tax preference is not achieved. Nor is the equity goal achieved, since payment of the individual income tax is concentrated in the top decile of income taxpayers in any case. Additionally, the revenue cost of the VAT credit is substantial—over 40 percent of estimated 1993 collections from the pre-reform system. The Project had recommended against the VAT credit and the medical deduction on efficiency and administrative grounds.

Taxation of Interest Income

The Project recommended that interest income be fully taxed. It was also recommended that Guatemala adopt a resident-based system of taxation and impose a tax on the worldwide income (both domestic and foreign-source at both the business and individual levels) earned by Guatemalan residents. Taxes paid abroad should be made creditable in Guatemala (Gersovitz 1987). The most significant change in the tax structure implied by this proposal is the full taxation of interest income.

There are a number of good reasons for bringing interest income into the tax base. First, taxation of interest income provides a revenue gain. Additionally, taxation of interest income moves toward the removal of the preference for debt finance and some distortions in investment decisions. Another benefit is that taxing interest income will increase the equity of the income tax because those who earn interest income tend to be in the higher income brackets.[11]

Some believe that the taxation of interest income will disproportionately hurt relatively low-income, small savers. There are ways to address this issue. One is to make up for the hardship by raising the standard deduction available to all income taxpayers. This would effectively eliminate the tax on low-income, small savers. Another is direct relief from income tax on interest income received by small savers. Special treatment may be required for pensioners. Some countries exclude a certain amount of interest income from taxable income (for examples, see Smith 1990a), but this has the disadvantage of greater administrative complexity. An increased standard deduction is probably easiest from an administrative standpoint. Whatever decision is made, it seems desirable to have the tax withheld by the lender. Herein lies one of the great advantages of the flat-rate tax over the progressive-rate tax. If the latter is used, the amount withheld by the bank will have to be allowed as credit for the total payment due from the individual taxpayer. This creates an administrative burden and gives the taxpayer a chance to escape payment on the remaining amount due. Many countries get around this problem by adopting a schedular system with interest income taxed at a differentially lower rate. The flat-rate tax allows the government to treat the interest tax as a straight withholding tax, and only those who do not use up the standard deduction with respect to all income will have to make use of the credit.

The issue of interest income taxation and capital flight is an important one. To assess the likelihood of capital flight as a response to the taxation of interest, it is particularly useful to consider the operation of the banking structure in Guatemala (Mutti 1991). The freeing of interest rates was not followed by a move to market rates of return. Rather, as reported by Brannon (1990), commercial banks only slightly raised rates paid on deposits, and the returns they offered were below those available on government saving instruments. Given high inflation rates and returns to depositors of 28 to 34 percent, real returns were decidedly negative. Correspondingly, real interest rates charged to borrowers were negative. The fact that such a decline in domestic rates of return has not been followed by an exodus of capital from Guatemala suggests that domestic and foreign investments are not perfect substitutes.

One explanation for this is that depositors hold funds in a commercial bank in order to qualify for loans made by that bank rather than pay the higher costs to enter the international capital market. The current negative cost of funds suggests that loans will be rationed, since the demand for funds is likely to exceed the available supply. Large depositors are willing to hold funds in a commercial bank because they receive a compensating benefit from loans below market costs. Hence for this group of depositors, taxing interest receipts can be thought of as increasing the cost of getting favorable access to bank credit or raising the cost to them of borrowing. Large-scale, capital flight does not occur because this is primarily an inframarginal adjustment, and the benefit from obtaining below-cost credit has been reduced but not eliminated.

The Guatemala government adopted a tax on interest income at a flat rate of 10 percent, which decidedly improves the efficiency of the tax. There is no income floor. It is levied as a withholding tax on banks, but there is no auditing of individual accounts because of the bank secrecy laws. It is estimated that the tax on interest income will increase revenues from the individual income tax by a significant amount. The projections for 1994 are that this change will net Q73 million, or about 18 percent of estimated collections under the pre-reform system (Table 5.4).

Taxation of All Bonuses

The Project recommended that all bonus income be taxed. If the intent of a bonus-exclusion policy is to give tax relief, then this should be done by the government through the tax system on a uniform basis for all employees. It is inappropriate to allow employers to determine the amounts and the recipients of tax relief. Either an increase in the standard deduction or a reduction in the general tax rate would offer a more equal benefit to all taxpayers. Under pre-reform practice, the bonus was an invitation to tax avoidance. Employers could at once deduct the bonus from taxable income under the company tax, and increase the take-home pay of employees with the tax-free bonus. The company gained by reducing its business income tax liability and, perhaps, by forgoing a larger regular wage increase to employees. Nonprofitable firms gained less because the deductibility of the bonus had no value to them, thus increasing the disparities in take-home pay among *types* of firms. The government consequently lost the revenue on both the individual income tax and the business income tax.[12]

The government decided to limit the tax-deductible Christmas bonus to the equivalent of one month's salary but to allow full deductibility of the bonus from business income tax liability. There was a relatively minor revenue consequence. The net effect was to tighten the rules on taxation of bonuses and reduce the tax avoidance issue somewhat.

Taxation of Life Insurance and Pensions

The Project recommended the taxation of pre-death distributions of life insurance benefits (net of premiums) and the taxation of received pension income (net of taxable contributions). Adoption of these recommendations would improve the equity of the system and would improve economic efficiency. Allowance of tax-free life insurance distributions creates an incentive to invest more heavily in life insurance for savings. As higher income individuals have more discretionary income to invest, the tax benefit accrues mostly to high-income individuals. The exclusion of pension income is sometimes defended on equity grounds. However, high-income individuals are likely to adjust portfolios to receive tax-free pension income, thus mitigating the equity argument.

A means-tested pension exclusion would be a better way to deal with the equity issue. The government rejected these proposals.

Taxation of Capital Gains

The Project recommended the taxation of capital gains income. The government adopted the recommendation and chose a rate of 15 percent. The tax is due when the returns are filed, and there is neither rate graduation nor deduction. The revenue consequences are relatively small.

Effects of the Reform Program

The structural changes to the individual income tax were estimated to yield lower revenue compared with the pre-reform system (Table 5.5). A relatively low top marginal rate was set, a liberal standard deduction allowed, and the VAT credit provided a substantial amount of taxpayer relief. The new schedular system taxes capital more at the individual level and at a slightly higher rate. With this reform, the individual income tax will play a less important role in the Guatemalan tax system in the future. For a discussion of the microsimulation models developed for this study, see Appendix A.

The Project estimated that revenues under the reformed system would be 50 percent lower by 1994 in comparison with what the pre-reform system would have yielded. By these estimates, a net of about 65,000 taxpayers would be dropped from the rolls, lessening the administrative burden of the tax. Over 80,000 taxpayers would see a reduction in their tax liability, and only 7,000 taxpayers would face an increase in their tax liability, largely due to the treatment of interest income. The overall burden of the tax would be reduced from the 0.5 percent of income of the pre-reform system to 0.3 percent under the reformed structure.[13] The reform does not significantly alter the distribution of tax burdens. All of the tax is paid by those in the top-income decile, and all of the tax reduction under this reform, therefore, accrues to this group (see Table 5.5). However, one might note that without this set of changes, some individuals with lower incomes would have eventually grown into the income-tax-paying population simply because of inflation and bracket creep. The reform increases the threshold, and restricts the tax net to those in the top income decile.

While the individual income tax reform has a revenue cost, it also has significant simplicity, efficiency, and horizontal equity benefits. The simplified rate structure and basic standard deduction (and elimination of other deductions) increase the administrative efficiency of the system.

The inclusion of other forms of income—interest, capital gains, and bonuses—increases the equity and efficiency of the system.[14]

However, a number of structural deficiencies continue to contribute to the complexity and inequalities of the system: the partial exclusion of the Christmas bonus and the preferential tax rate on capital gains and interest income result in unequal treatment of taxpayers who derive their income from different sources. As discussed earlier, these differential rates lead to efficiency losses. These differences also distort the horizontal equity of the system. There is the potential to include these in the tax base at a later time, but it is rather unlikely.[15]

The lack of indexation in the reform will cause the structure to lose its progressivity over time, *or* it will encourage annual adjustments to the rate brackets to adjust for inflationary increases in income and tax liability. In either case, the effective tax structure will likely change over time, thus altering the intended effects of the reform. Legislated indexation of the system could help to maintain the goals of the reform. True indexation has been relatively successful in Mexico and Columbia (Burgess and Stern 1993).

The VAT credit is not an effective policing mechanism. As discussed by Tait (1988), the requirement of an invoice for the individual income tax credit may simply increase the incidence of counterfeit invoices. As it stands, the credit is treated as an additional standard deduction. Simplicity of the system could be enhanced by simply expanding the standard deduction or by dropping the VAT credit.

Notes

1. Parts of this chapter draw heavily from Thuronyi (1990), Martinez-Vazquez (1989), and Galper and Ramos (1992).

2. A detailed administrative reform package is described in Austin (1989), Martinez-Vazquez (1989), Coburn (1990), and Stacey (1989c).

3. Thuronyi (1990) provides more detail on this issue.

4. Proponents of a flat-rate tax list the following among the benefits of a single-rate structure: reduced incentive for evasion, simplicity, and increased economic efficiency (Hall and Rabushka 1995; Alm, Bahl, and Murray 1991a).

5. More detail on deductions is presented in Martinez-Vazquez (1989) and Thuronyi (1990).

6. Another benefit, known as the "incentive-increase" was exempt from tax to the employee and is deductible by the employer. This benefit, established by *Decreto* no. 78-89, was fixed at a minimum of Q0.30 per hour on a temporary basis until the amount of increase was agreed on between employers and workers (Thuronyi 1990, pp.31-32).

7. As noted in Bird (1989, 1992) a flat-rate tax may not be appropriate in cases where the true target for revenue is a higher income group.

8. The projections for 1992-1994 presented in Tables 5.4 and 5.5 were made by KPMG using a microsimulation model. They assume no change in compliance rate and no behavioral response to changes in the tax system. The underlying economic assumptions of the projections are presented in appendix Table A. The models used are described in Bachrach and Covert (1992), Bachrach and Mizrahi (1993), Greaney, Mizrahi and Covert (1992a, 1992b), Newland and Beckwith (1992a, 1992b), and Vasquez, Madrigal and Greaney (1989). The detailed results are presented in Bahl, Martinez-Vazquez, and Wallace (1994).

9. In recent years, this same reasoning has been used in Jamaica (Alm, Bahl and Murray 1991a) and Colombia (McLure and Santiago 1992) to replace personal allowances with a standard deduction.

10. A similar scheme was adopted in Turkey (Tait 1988, pp. 283-84). While giving a VAT credit gives low-income individuals some relief from the tax, this credit is allowed for *all* taxpayers, thereby mitigating its distributional benefit. An alternative credit aimed specifically at low-income individuals would better serve the regressivity issue associated with the VAT, but would not necessarily aid compliance. Such credits for *sales* taxes are often used in the United States (Fox 1995).

11. This is pointed out by Musgrave (1984), who also contends that the best that may be said about a preference for tax saving is that the preferential treatment of savings may redirect investment from informal markets to organized savings institutions (p. 255).

12. Such deductions were rampant in Jamaica before their 1986 reform. That reform also reduced the number of deductible bonuses (Bahl 1991b).

13. For more information on the derivation of these incidence results, see Galper and Ramos (1992).

14. These base-broadening reforms were also seen in Mexico (1987-1990), Columbia (1986-1988), Jamaica (1986), and Indonesia (1983-1986). See Burgess and Stern (1993).

15. For example, in Jamaica, a number of exemptions have crept back into the system.

6

Company Income Tax: Proposals and Reform

The income tax on companies was an important component of the Guatemalan system, accounting for about 25 percent of tax revenues in 1991, but the level of company income taxation was not high.[1] Even though the corporate income tax was relatively small, it had important potential and real effects on investment decisions and on the choice of production techniques. In fact, Guatemalan company income tax law prior to the reform was not consistent with the government's objectives of equity, efficiency, and simplicity. Many of the problems arose from the faulty integration of company and personal income taxes, repeating in Guatemala the experience of many other countries in this region. Before the reform, capital income in the form of dividends, capital gains, and interest was exempt or lightly taxed at the individual level, primarily as a result of exclusions from the tax base. In effect, this made the personal income tax similar to a consumption-based tax. In addition, at the corporate level, shareholder income was often untaxed because certain important components of company income were untaxed. Incomes from nationally promoted activities (such as exports, tourism, industry) were exempt. Also, interest and other costs incurred to earn tax-exempt income were de facto deducted as expenses, even though there was a source rule that required costs such as interest to be deducted only if taxable income was earned.

The enforcement of the company income tax had also been a serious problem. Traditionally, few resources were devoted to audit. In addition, penalty assessments were low and not frequently applied. As a result, many companies did not pay corporate income tax, leading to failure in another objective for company income taxation: adequate revenue raising. Company income tax collections in 1990 were Q300.5 million, an amount

equivalent to less than 1 percent of GDP. The different levels of enforcement and compliance also meant de facto different effective rates of
taxation, adding distortions and horizontal inequities.

The Pre-reform System

The company income tax was levied on stock corporations, limited
liability companies, general partnerships, limited partnerships, and
partnerships limited by shares. Sole proprietorships were taxed under the
personal income tax. Guatemala followed a territorial principle of
taxation. That is, foreign-source income earned by entities operating in
Guatemala was not taxed, and no credit was given for taxes paid abroad.

Two important categories of income were tax-exempt: (1) interest on
deposits held with regulated financial institutions, high quality bonds,
and market-traded bonds; and (2) intercompany dividend and profit
shares, if the distributing entity had paid company tax. Realized capital
gains on property assets were in principle taxed as ordinary income, but
the law provided sufficient qualifications and loopholes to effectively
eliminate any tax on capital gains. Income earned on long-term contracts
also received special treatment. Companies could elect to report all
income the year the asset was transferred or attribute income to earlier
periods, based on the percentage of work done.

The tax required most companies to maintain accounts using the
accrual method. An important exception to this general rule was for
financial institutions regulated by the Superintendent of Banks (banks,
insurance companies, and other regulated financial companies).[2] These
companies were required by the superintendent to report revenues on a
cash rather than an accrual method. But the financial companies were
permitted to use accrual methods for reporting interest expenses. As a
result, revenues and expenses of regulated financial institutions were
mismatched, and companies could claim expenses prior to the actual
receipt of the revenues from the transaction.

Interest incurred in producing income was deductible from the
company income tax, subject to certain limitations: interest incurred on
debt used to finance tax-exempt activities was not deductible, and interest
expenses could not be deducted at a rate greater than the maximum bank
rate. However, both limitations were actually ineffective.

Foreign exchange losses incurred to produce Guatemalan-source
income were also deductible. However, this deduction did not apply to
transactions made by branches, subsidiaries, and agencies of foreign
companies with a head office located abroad. Given the devaluations of
the quetzal, foreign exchange losses were quite substantial for many

companies in the pre-reform period. Foreign exchange gains on Guatemalan-source income were considered by the tax law as part of taxable income. However, in practice, foreign transactions could have been arranged in a way to make foreign exchange capital gains effectively tax-exempt.

Because of the troublesome history of compliance, the tax law contained a number of enforcement provisions. In addition to withholding personal income tax on employees' wages and salaries, withholding taxes were applied to certain forms of capital income. Royalties, rents, and non-exempt interest had a withholding tax of 4 percent. In addition, several limitations were imposed on the ability of companies to use deductions. Companies had the obligation to apportion costs between taxable and non-taxable activities due to tax incentives. Other limitations involved payments to spouses and directors, royalties, and travel costs. The law also gave the tax administration the authority to use presumptive methods of income determination for the taxpayers who did not file a tax return or who failed to produce the necessary information during an audit.

The corporate income tax had a progressive statutory tax rate structure. After the 1987 reform, the rates for the corporate tax became 12 percent for companies with income less than Q30,000, 22 percent for companies with income of Q30,000-60,000, and 34 percent for companies with income more than Q60,000. These tax rates were not applied in a step fashion but instead to the entire taxable income of the company. Thus if a company had over Q60,000 in taxable profits, a rate of 34 percent applied also to all profits up to Q60,000.

Composition of the Tax Base

The percentage distribution of the companies by standard industry classification is shown in Table 2.4. Most companies subject to the corporate income tax were in the trade sector (31 percent of all companies). The fewest number of firms were in the mining and petroleum sector (less than 1 percent). The alternative distribution of companies according to asset size is shown in Table 2.5. As is typical of tax structures in many other countries, the largest number of companies in Guatemala were at the low end of asset size. In 1992, 91 percent of the companies had assets under 5 million quetzals. However, the remaining 9 percent of the (taxpaying) companies represented 65 percent of all corporate income tax collections. About 45 percent of companies were in the tax-loss position (negative taxable income), with another 36 percent in the two smallest taxable income ranges (0-5,000 and 5,000-23,000 quetzals). Less than one-quarter of 1 percent of companies were in the 2 million-and-over taxable income range. By industry groups, it is especially notable that more than one-half of companies were in a tax-loss position in several sectors: mining, construction, and trade and services. This extraordinary number of companies in the tax-loss or low-income position suggested that a considerable amount of taxable income was either legally excluded from taxation due to tax holidays, or it went illegally unreported. According to Guatemalan tax administration authorities, this profile was typical of what they had confronted for many years: most companies declared losses for tax purposes. Massive tax evasion was suspected because it was unlikely that so many companies could be so unprofitable for such a long period of time and remain open for business.

The role of tax holidays and incentives on the narrow base of the corporate income tax is documented in Table 3.6. This table produces estimates of the tax expenditures—or foregone revenues—arising from tax incentive and tax holiday provisions in the pre-reform system. In particular, this table shows the foregone revenues from three features of the pre-reform company tax: the interest income exemption, tax rates below the maximum 34 percent, and the education incentive deduction. Under previous law, the interest income exemption reduced company tax liabilities in 1992 by Q51.0 million. The most important tax expenditure from tax incentives came from the industrial decentralization credit which reduced revenues by Q43 million in 1992. Table 3.6 also shows that many other tax incentives in the pre-reform regime had a negligible impact on revenues (measured for 1992) and were not widely used.

Problems and Reform Issues

The previous company tax was beset by a number of problems that arose from both its structure and its enforcement.[3] The most important of these problems were these: tax treatment of interest income and the feasibility of a consumption-based income tax; integration of the individual and corporate income taxes; treatment of capital gains; fringe benefits for workers; timing issues, including depreciation and inventory valuation; tax incentives; inflation adjustments; the taxation of foreign enterprises, foreign tax credit issues, and income earned abroad by Guatemalan companies; the tax treatment of financial institutions; and the tax rate schedule.

Tax Treatment of Interest

The exemption of interest income earned on bank deposits and marketed bonds under the previous corporate income tax implied that most interest income tax was exempt at both the personal and company levels. Moreover, interest at the company level was deductible. The deductibility of interest at the company level and exemption of interest at the personal level allowed company income to be distributed free of tax to investors in the form of interest income, in addition to allowing the company a deduction for the paid interest. This tax structure also allowed companies to engage in arbitrage by borrowing tax-deductible funds to invest in securities with interest earnings that were tax-exempt.

The benefit to companies of being able to deduct interest costs was increased manyfold at high inflation rates. Because inflation erodes the real value of the debt, the nominal interest cost incurred by a firm includes a premium to compensate lenders for the loss in purchasing power. As a result, nominal interest deductions unadjusted for inflation allowed a company to deduct not only real interest but part of the loan principal. Actually, at high rates of inflation, the deduction of all interest costs may have led to negative marginal effective rates of taxation (METRs),[4] i.e., a subsidy from the treasury at the Ministry of Finance to taxpaying companies. (This subsidy is not a direct cash subsidy but instead the taxpayer's ability to pay less corporate tax or other taxes because of the excess deduction for interest costs.) The issue of inflation adjustment is addressed later on in the context of overall indexing for inflation. Here the focus is on the asymmetry introduced in the previous corporate income tax by the exemption of interest income and the full deduction allowance for interest costs.

There are two methods for handling the asymmetry problem. The first is to broaden the company and personal tax to include all interest income, thus allowing interest to be deducted without limitation. In this case, the company tax is effectively a withholding tax on income accruing to shareholders, since interest costs are deductible from company income. The other option is to allow interest income to be tax-exempt but to disallow the deductibility of interest costs at both the company and individual level. This approach would mean that the company income tax applies to profits (gross of net interest deductions) and serves as a withholding tax on income accruing to both shareholders and bondholders.

Overall, there are more advantages to the first approach of taxing all interest income and allowing full deductibility of interest cost. This method facilitates the crediting of the Guatemalan company tax in the home countries of foreign companies operating in Guatemala. Taxing interest income at the company and individual levels also eliminates tax-planning opportunities and increases the horizontal equity of the tax system. Making all interest income taxable may create a disincentive to savings. However, the evidence from other countries where this issue has been studied in much detail suggests that the impact on overall aggregate savings may be small.

A Consumption-Based Cash-Flow Tax

An entirely different approach to the treatment of interest income would be to adopt consumption tax approach to income taxation in Guatemala.[5] A consumption-based tax has not yet been adopted by any other country although it often has been analyzed as a serious alternative to comprehensive income taxes.[6] The structure of a conventional consumption-based tax allows individuals to deduct deposits into registered savings accounts and adds to the tax base withdrawals from those savings accounts (dissavings). Interest income accumulates tax free until this income is withdrawn from the account.

Monitoring account registration in this framework could be cumbersome. An alternative design of a consumption-based tax allows individuals to hold tax-exempt, nonregistered savings accounts in which deposits are not deductible but in which neither withdrawals nor interest income is taxable. In effect, this approach allows taxes on future withdrawals to be prepaid. However, the approach with nonregistered accounts requires a company cash-flow tax. This tax, in effect, withholds taxes on the personal consumption of shareholders from those returns to investment that earn above-normal rates of return. The investment in a company can be defined either as a deposit into a registered or nonregistered account.

The tax base of a cash-flow tax is the difference between revenues and current expenditures on wages, materials, *and* capital purchases. No deductions for depreciation or interest are allowed, since the full expensing for capital is equivalent to deducting the economic cost of depreciation and the financing costs from the tax base (whether this is the imputed cost of equity finance or debt-financing costs). From an efficiency viewpoint the cash-flow tax has significant advantages. It eliminates any possible distortions caused by inflation in the measurement of income (all computations are performed at current money values), and it may be more conducive to savings and investment because with a cash-flow tax, the marginal effective rate of taxation on investment is in effect zero. Despite these advantages, it was deemed early in the reform process that a consumption-based income tax with a cash-flow treatment of companies would not be politically feasible in Guatemala. One big disadvantage was that the consumption tax would tax wage and salary income more heavily than it would other types of income, and this was a problem that the government was supposed to address. Two other factors weighed heavily against this option: first, no other country had actually introduced this type of tax, and second, this type of tax may not be credited to foreign companies doing business in Guatemala by their home-country tax administrations.

Integration of Company and Individual Income Taxes

Better integration of personal and company income taxes on income accruing to shareholders was an important tax reform consideration.[7] The issue was to avoid as best as possible the double taxation of income from profits, which can be taxed once at the corporate level and again at the individual level.

An integration approach to individual and company income taxation views company taxation as a withholding tax of individual income at the company level. Generally, it is possible to distinguish between partial (dividend only) or full (dividends and retained earnings) integration methods. Three partial integration options were considered. The first would use the "imputation" system that is familiar in many European countries and Canada. The idea of the imputation system is to gross-up income received by the shareholder to reflect the company tax paid by the company. The shareholder pays taxes on the grossed-up value of income but is then given a credit equal to the underlying company taxes paid prior to distribution of income. The imputation system has a number of desirable features, especially with respect to eliminating tax-planning opportunities for owners of closely held companies. However, the imputation systems adopted throughout the world have tended to deal with the distribution of dividend income to the neglect of shareholder income arising from capital gains generated by the reinvestment of profits.

A serious limitation to the possible use of the imputation system in Guatemala was the significant reporting requirements. It is important that each taxpayer be informed by the company of the grossed-up value of dividends received and the amount of the dividend tax credit that could be used to reduce taxes paid. When the taxpayers filed, both the grossed-up value of dividends and the dividend tax credit would be reported. To audit the amounts, the government would have to check that the grossed-up value of dividends claimed by each taxpayer matched the amount declared by the company.

A second option would have allowed dividends to be deducted from the company tax base and fully taxed as part of income received by the shareholder. This option was not appealing for two reasons: the compliance and reporting requirements are problematic, and the deductibility of dividends would have caused a considerable loss in tax revenues earned from dividends remitted to nonresidents.

The third option is similar to the integration approach used in pre-reform Guatemala. Dividends and capital gains could be exempt at the personal level. If the company income tax were levied at the top personal tax rate and economic income were taxed, integration would be roughly achieved at least for the higher income owners of the company. Under a flat-rate system integration would be achieved for nearly all share-holders.

Full integration can be achieved in two ways. Under the partnership method, company profits are fully imputed to stockholders and they are taxed only once under the individual income tax. Under the capital gain method, full integration is achieved through the taxation of all capital gains (including unrealized capital gains) and the simultaneous repeal of company taxation. Neither of the two full-integration approaches were considered practical for Guatemala. Of the three partial-integration approaches, the personal exemption method seemed the most feasible.

Taxation of Capital Gains

The pre-reform corporate income tax-exempted capital gains on the sale of shares owned by a company. This was consistent with the partial integration of individual and corporate income taxes. In addition, capital gains arising from the sale of nondepreciable assets were included in income on an installment basis over a period of three years. This installment method conferred an unwarranted tax advantage to taxpayers because they could defer the payment of capital gains over time, thereby significantly reducing their tax liabilities in inflationary times. These capital gains should be fully included in income in the year they are realized. However, it was decided that capital gains on intercorporate shares should remain tax-exempt. Since the company that issues the shares is taxable, an additional capital gains tax to be paid by another company that purchases and sells shares would have been a form of double taxation.

Fringe Benefits for Workers

Before the reform, companies were permitted to deduct contributions to pension funds, insurance policies, and expenditures on employee housing under industrial promotion programs. These contributions, however, were not treated as taxable fringe benefits received by workers. As in many other countries, for tax purposes labor compensation in the form of fringe benefits was treated more favorably in Guatemala than was wage income. To deal with this problem two options were considered. The first allowed a company to deduct the cost of fringe benefits at the same time the fringe benefits were included in taxable personal income of employees. This required a withholding tax on fringe benefits similar to that for wage income. Of course, if the worker were to earn income below the standard deduction, the amount of tax withheld on both wages and fringe benefits would be zero.

The second option was to deny the company the deduction and exempt the fringe benefit from taxation at the personal level. This approach is inferior to the former option (under any income tax structure but a unified flat-rate tax), since the denial of the deduction assumes that the fringe benefit is paid to a worker who is taxed at the same rate as the company.

Depreciation Expenses

Pre-reform depreciation allowances were generally based on straight-line methods, with rates varying by type of asset. It is unclear how closely these rates reflected economic depreciation. Assets with lives longer than those prescribed benefited from relatively fast deductions. (This appears to have been the case with most types of machinery.) On the other hand, since there was no indexation of the original cost of the asset for inflation, depreciation deductions may have been inadequate relative to the cost of replacing the asset. Given Guatemala's previous experience with high inflation rates, this was and remains an important problem.

One option considered was the simplification of the pre-reform treatment of depreciation expenses by moving to a "pooled class" for depreciation allowance as opposed to the "individual asset" approach used at the time. The "pooled class" concept works as follows: Assets are aggregated into various classes, depending on their rate of depreciation (e.g., 5 percent for buildings; 10 percent for ships and railroad rolling stock, furniture, and equipment; 20 percent for machinery and vehicles, and so on). When an expenditure is made on the purchase of a particular type of asset, the value of the expenditure is included in the undepreciated capital cost base of the current year for that particular class or type of asset. Depreciation is calculated by a declining-balance method. The declining-balance rate is applied to the aggregate value of the undepreciated capital-cost base of the entire asset class.

The other issues considered were the depreciation method and rates. The pre-reform straight-line depreciation rates were too generous, especially for buildings (20-year life), machinery (5-year life), and ships and railroads (10-year life). One possibility considered was switching from straight-line to declining-balance methods. If this method were adopted, the values of depreciation deduction could be effectively halved. These rates of depreciation would then correspond more closely to the true economic life of the asset.

Inventory Valuation

The method of inventory valuation under the previous corporate income tax allowed companies to write off costs based on the price of the last item added to the inventory. Because all interest unadjusted for inflation was fully deductible, this treatment of inventory costs was too generous. Effectively, companies were allowed to deduct the inflationary increase of inventory values and, in addition, they were allowed to deduct debt-financing costs unadjusted for inflation. This meant that companies were allowed a double deduction for inflation for inventory investment.

An alternative considered was the use of first-in, first-out (FIFO) methods of valuation with a deduction from taxable income for inventory costs to recognize inflation. This inventory deduction would be set as a percentage of the inventory balance over the year. This percentage could be set as a proportion of the inflation rate to recognize the ability of the company to finance part of its inventory with debt. For example, if a company were to finance one-third of its capital with debt, then the inventory allowance would be two-thirds of the rate of inflation.

If, on the other hand, interest deductions were indexed for inflation, the inventory adjustment for inflation could be modified as follows. The inventories would be valued according to FIFO accounting techniques, but the inventory allowance would be set equal to the rate of inflation.

Long-Term Contracts

Under the pre-reform corporate income tax, companies engaged in the construction industry could report income on a completed contract basis or when the income was actually received. The latter allowed companies to report income years after the deductions had been taken. This mismatch of income and expenses conferred a tax advantage to a company. One option considered was to require the "completed contract" method for all companies. This method requires a company to report income each year according to the percentage of the project that has been completed during that year. A second option considered was to require companies to capitalize interest, depreciation, and other costs during the life of the contract in the value of the asset. If the asset were sold, those costs could be deducted from the sale price of the asset.

Cost of Resource Exploitation

The pre-reform corporate income tax law contained special provisions that applied to companies engaged in forestry, mining, and petroleum activities. Depletion allowances for forest exploitation were allowed as a deduction, which was calculated as the amount of output produced times the production costs per unit of estimated reserves. Allowable costs included concession fees but excluded the cost of land and depreciable fixed assets. No depletion deduction was permitted for mining and petroleum activities. However, mining companies were permitted to expense exploration costs in a single period or in five equal and consecutive installments after the start of production. Petroleum companies were also allowed to expense all exploration and exploitation costs. These provisions were relatively generous because enterprises were able to write off expenses prior to earning resource income in later years.

The main option considered for reform was the special deduction for the cost of resource exploitation for mining and petroleum companies. A simple method that would avoid mismatching income and expenses in the previous law would be to allow the deduction of a depletion allowance based on the capitalized value of exploration and development expenses. The cost would be calculated as the capitalized exploration and development expenses divided by estimated reserves of the mineral times actual production. This deduction would be similar to the depletion cost allowed forestry companies.

Treatment of Losses

The pre-reform corporate income tax law did not allow a deduction for prior operating losses. (That is, no loss carryforwards were allowed.) The law did not allow the carryback of losses. In addition, as a general rule, unused deductions could not be carried forward to later years. Such restrictions made it difficult for companies with fluctuating income to smooth out their lumpy earnings. This treatment penalized, in particular, certain types of activities such as the construction industry, characterized by uneven activity flows. The restrictions also penalized companies with riskier or more uneven net income flows. These companies "shared" their profits with the government in good times but did not receive any tax relief when losses were incurred. Nevertheless, some of the negative impact was partially offset by provisions in the corporate income tax law that allowed taxpayers to improve the matching income and expenses, such as the completed contract method and different valuation techniques for inventories.

Several options for reform were considered in this area. Clearly, some liberalization of tax loss carryforwards would have reduced the need for a number of provisions in the tax law geared to allow companies to smooth out taxable income. These provisions included the tax treatment of capital gains on an installment basis over three years, different methods used to value income for long-term contracts, and different valuation techniques for inventories. One simple reform option would be to allow tax losses to be carried forward for three years, with special provisions remaining for agriculture and natural resource companies. After improvement in the administration and enforcement of the company tax, the loss carryforward provision could be extended to more years and perhaps a limited loss carryback provision could be introduced.

Tax Incentives

A number of tax incentives, mainly in the form of deductions, credits, or income tax holidays, were granted to companies operating in Guatemala under the pre-reform corporate income tax.[8] Several special incentives were granted to new investments. A general incentive for industrial promotion allowed large companies to expense 10 percent (20 percent for small companies) of the cost of qualifying new machinery. In addition, construction companies were allowed to deduct the cost of dwellings provided for workers, and forestry companies were allowed to take a credit for all costs incurred during the first eight years of reforestation work. All credits were limited to 50 percent of the income tax liability in any year. Companies were also allowed to get a credit for the social security payments for new workers (over and above those employed during the previous year) earning less than Q500 per month. This credit also had a limit of 50 percent of the company tax liability in any year for companies located in the department of Guatemala. For companies located in other departments the limit was 100 percent of the tax liability.

From a revenue viewpoint, the most important company income tax expenditures were the full or partial exemption of income arising from promoted activities. These tax holidays were granted on a permanent or temporary basis. Ten-year tax holidays were granted to companies involved in milk and Indian rubber production and in export promotion. Those manufacturing companies with at least 30 workers and with at least 50 percent Guatemalan control operating outside Guatemala City were granted 70 percent exemption for 8 years, or 80 percent for 8 years, or 90 percent for 10 years, depending on a number of quantifying characteristics. Small manufacturing companies with fewer than 30 workers and real assets below Q50,000 were granted an exemption from income tax ranging from 80 percent to 100 percent, for 10 years. All companies engaged in tourism activities were granted a 2-year income tax holiday. The pre-reform tax law also granted a 15-year income tax holiday for enterprises operating export zones. These generous and complex fiscal incentives reduced revenues significantly and introduced severe distortions. Their rationalization was a high priority in the reform agenda.

Inflation Adjustments

The experience of Guatemala with high inflation made it important to assess different options for the indexation of the income tax. To index company income, a number of adjustments were required.

Inflation may result in distortions in taxpayer economic decisions, unless some adjustment for price increases is introduced. Ideally a tax system will be inflation-neutral when in real terms the tax base is the same with zero or any positive rate of inflation. Distortions and differential real taxation take place because some revenues or costs are measured at current nominal prices, and others are measured at nominal historical costs.

Inflation adjustment requires the more familiar adjustment in the historical value of capital assets and inventories but also the less familiar adjustment of liabilities for inflation-induced declines in the real value of the taxpayer's debt.[9]

Two methods have been used to adjust income taxes for inflation. The most widely used adjusts individual items in the net income computation. The most important individual items to be adjusted include depreciation allowances, valuation of inventories, interest deductions:

- The undepreciated capital costs of depreciable assets have to be increased by the rate of inflation each year. Under either the "individual" or "pooled asset" approach for depreciation, indexation could easily be accomplished by multiplying the cost basis of the asset by 1 plus the rate of inflation and carrying forward this amount to the next year for the calculation of depreciation.

- The cost-basis of inventories, depletable assets, and capitalized expenditures (long-term contracts) and nondepreciable assets could be increased by the general rate of inflation. Inventories could be valued according to first-in, first-out accounting methods. The value of the cost basis of the inventory, however, would be increased from one year to the next by the rate of inflation. For depletion costs, the value of exploration and development expenditures used to calculate depletion would be increased by the inflation rate each year to measure the cost of depletion. Income earned on long-term contracts would be calculated as the difference between the sale price of an asset and the capitalized expenditures indexed for inflation. Capital gains earned on the sale of nondepreciable assets would be calculated as the difference between the sale price and the original cost indexed for inflation.

- To the extent that interest would be deductible, an adjustment for interest costs would be required to reduce deductions by the inflation component of interest rates. This adjustment would be made to the net financial liabilities of the company (debt liabilities net of financial assets). Net financial liabilities would be calculated by aggregating short- and long-term bonds, loans, and mortgages, and subtracting these from financial assets, including cash, demand and term deposits, and other interest-earning assets held at the beginning of the year. The net financial liabilities then would be multiplied by the rate of inflation to arrive at the interest deductions that would be disallowed.

The partial indexation against inflation can introduce distortions of its own. Partial adjustments can de facto subsidize some types of assets or income and at the same time penalize others. These problems are avoided with the second method for indexation, which is the comprehensive adjustment for inflation of the entire balance sheet. This method allows us to derive from the adjusted balance sheet an inflation-adjusted profit as the tax base. This approach offers the advantage that it also adjusts for inflation the tax bases of other taxes such as those on capital gains and net worth. In countries where there has been pervasive inflation, such as Chile, Israel, Brazil and Argentina, complete adjustment to inflation has involved the adjustment of the entire balance sheet to real terms. Different but largely equivalent accounting methods have been used.

In either type of indexation, partial or full, several transition issues would need to be addressed.[10] Also, if company profits were adjusted for inflation, it would also be important to introduce several of these adjustments at the personal level, especially for capital gains, interest income, and borrowing costs. All things considered, given the difficulties with tax enforcement and the relatively weak accounting practices in the country, the options actually considered for reform involved only partial adjustments for inflation. Full indexation would have complicated the tax administration system, perhaps to a degree that could not be accommodated in Guatemala at the time of the reform. Moreover, full indexation might have eroded the revenue elasticity of the revenue system at a time when inflation was pushing up expenditure requirements. In addition, full indexation might have been interpreted politically as giving in to the inevitability of chronic inflation.

Ad hoc methods of inflation adjustments also would avoid adjusting interest income and interest expenses for inflation, which were deemed likely to fail in Guatemala. The two adjustments considered were for inventory valuation and depreciation allowances. To compensate for the lack of adjustment of interest cost deductions, both inventory valuation and depreciation adjustments needed a share of the inflation rate used for indexation, which would reflect the debt leverage of the firm. For example, if a company financed 75 percent of its capital by debt, the inflation adjustment would be one-quarter of the rate of inflation times the cost base of the asset. For nondepreciable property and depletable assets, a similar adjustment for the cost basis of assets would be required.

Taxation of Income Earned Abroad by Guatemalans

The government considered a shift from the territorial method to the residence method of taxing foreign-source income.[11] Under the territorial method, foreign-source income was exempt from taxation. Under the residence method, foreign-source income would be taxable with relief given for foreign taxes paid.

The territoriality principle complemented the pre-reform treatment of capital income in Guatemala. Since much of capital income earned on domestic investments was exempt from taxation in Guatemala, the exemption of foreign-source earnings, presumably for the most part income from capital, was consistent with that treatment of domestic-source capital income. But if Guatemala were to tax all capital income, including interest earned in Guatemala, then it would be quite appropriate to shift to a residence-based method of taxation. Taxing domestic interest income without taxing passive investment income from investments abroad could lead to a large outflow of capital from Guatemala, as long as there is some substitutability between foreign and domestic assets.[12]

Taxing domestic interest income but not foreign interest income would also present problems of horizontal equity (taxpayers with the same income would not be treated equally) and could lead to tax evasion. Both evasion control and equity considerations pointed toward the adoption of a worldwide system of income taxation. This residence-based or worldwide method would include either a foreign tax credit that would be deductible from Guatemala taxes and payable on foreign-source income or a deduction of foreign taxes from foreign taxable income in Guatemala. The advantage of the foreign tax credit is that companies locating in Guatemala would not be at a disadvantage in earning foreign-source income by paying more taxes than would otherwise be paid on Guatemalan-source income. The deduction method on the other hand leads to double taxation of foreign-source income.

It is important to point out that the Guatemalan territorial system of the pre-reform corporate income tax was more generous than the territorial systems applied by many other countries. This is so because both active and passive income were exempt from Guatemalan tax, while most countries exempt only active business income. An alternative approach considered for Guatemala would provide territorial treatment for active operating income of Guatemalan firms and residents but make passive investment income subject to Guatemalan tax.

Either proposal would represent a major change in Guatemalan tax policy if it were to be enforced effectively, because it would require steps to exchange taxpayer information with foreign countries. To date Guatemala had signed no foreign treaties, nor had it sought to reach less comprehensive agreements regarding taxpayer information exchanges. Becoming a party to such types of agreements would require changes in Guatemalan financial practices, particularly the reliance on bearer share ownership of public companies.

Taxation of Foreign Enterprises in Guatemala

Taxation of foreign enterprises operating in Guatemala under the pre-reform corporate income tax also followed a territorial method of taxation.[13] This system was designed to tax income generated in Guatemala, regardless of the residence of the individual or firm generating this income. Consistent with this goal, foreign firms operating in Guatemala generally were subject to the same company tax laws as domestic firms. Primary differences in the treatment of foreign and domestic firms arose over the imposition of withholding taxes on remittances to foreigners and the determination of presumptive income in certain industries.

Such withholding taxes often are justified as final payment in lieu of levying a personal level tax on the eventual recipient of Guatemalan-source income. But given that dividends and interest were mostly free of tax at the personal level within Guatemala, such a rationale was not applicable. Rather, the motivation for withholding taxes on foreign businesses operating in Guatemala seemed most directly related to the rationale offered in residence-based, or worldwide, systems of taxation: Guatemala has the opportunity to extract rents from foreigners, either from foreign owners of businesses operating in Guatemala or from foreign treasuries. When foreign-controlled businesses earn monopoly profits by serving protected domestic markets or when their returns represent a gain from applying a particular technology or introducing a particular product whose costs of development already are sunk, then rents are being earned by foreigners, and a tax imposed on those rents will have little influence on the firm's current price and production decisions. Alternatively, if the home country of the foreign investor taxes worldwide income of its residents but offers a credit for foreign income taxes paid, then the Guatemalan treasury gains revenue at the expense of the treasury in the home country. Such opportunities to gain revenue without appreciably increasing tax burdens are particular attractive.

Guatemalan pre-reform company tax included the following withholding taxes for non-residents: If interest was paid to non-residents (except financial institutions), a 25 percent withholding tax rate applied. If dividends or branch profits were remitted, a 12.5 percent withholding tax rate was levied. This implied a 42 percent effective tax rate on dividends if the company was in the 34 percent category; 32 percent for a company tax rate of 22 percent; 23 percent for a company in the 12 percent category; and 12.5 percent for non-taxpaying companies.

The final impact of the withholding taxes that are imposed on interest and dividend income earned by foreigners will depend upon two factors. First, whether foreign lenders are subject to taxation in their home countries on their foreign-source income. And second, whether and which Guatemalan taxes will be creditable in the home country. At the time of the reform there was a sizeable group of foreign-controlled enterprises operating in Guatemala that clearly treated the Guatemala tax as the final tax due on their Guatemalan income. These enterprises originated in countries, such as Mexico and certain Western European countries, that exempt earnings from foreign operations. Many other enterprises were from countries like the United States that used a residence-based method of taxation that generally would give a credit for taxes paid in Guatemala.

Although dividends and interest payments were the major income flows received by foreigners in Guatemala, other items subject to withholding included royalties, payments for technical assistance, and other types of service income. For some specific categories of service income earned by foreigners, including those in the film distribution, insurance, transportation, and communication industries, the pre-reform income tax levied a withholding tax in the form of a share of gross receipts.

The withholding tax on dividend payments to foreigners at a rate of 12.5 percent did not seem to provide a major deterrent to investment in Guatemala and could be kept in place. However, the combined income and withholding tax burden on dividends paid to foreign owners was likely to generate excess foreign tax credits for U.S. parent firms. Under those circumstances, any reduction in Guatemalan tax would yield a benefit to the U.S. investor, not the U.S. Treasury. Thus, any Guatemalan tax reduction could affect the location of new investment from countries using a residence principle. Tax reductions could also affect the level of the investment from countries using a territorial principle of taxation.

One of the urgent issues for consideration of reform was the adjustment of the high withholding rate on interest income paid to foreigners. The pre-reform withholding tax of 25 percent on interest income needed to be reduced to a rate no higher than 20 percent. While the pre-reform rate effectively discouraged foreign affiliates from borrowing from their parents—generally a desirable goal—it also raised the cost of debt to other private borrowers. Perhaps as a result, most foreign borrowing was channelled through the Bank of Guatemala, which allowed the subsequent debt service payments to be tax-exempt. Movement toward a more market-oriented allocation of loanable funds would call for a reduction in the withholding rate on interest payments to foreigners.

A further aspect of withholding tax policy that needed to be reassessed was the set of presumptive income tax rates levied on foreign providers of certain services, and their discriminatory treatment vis-à-vis, domestic providers of similar services. Withholding rates on other sources of income also needed to be reduced to no more than 20 percent. There was also a need to consider the introduction of apportionment formulas that improved the linkage between tax bases to net income. The withholding taxes may have been introduced with the goal of protecting domestic producers who faced much lower tax burdens. But in this case, the effectiveness of such policies should have been reevaluated periodically. Supposedly, the objective of the policy was to allow a Guatemalan business to establish itself in an industry where it could learn by doing and eventually compete effectively with foreigner producers. The objective of the policy was not to encourage inefficient production by firms that always will require protection in order to survive.

Treatment of Financial Institutions

Under the pre-reform corporate income tax, regulated financial institutions (banks and insurance companies) were permitted to treat income on a cash basis.[14] In addition, loan interest received by regulated financial companies was generally tax-exempt. However, a minimum tax was imposed on financial institutions. This tax required the company to include tax-exempt income as part of its taxable income for minimum tax purposes. The rate of the minimum tax was 18 percent. The financial company paid the greater of the company income tax or the minimum tax.

As a pseudo-tax, banks and insurance companies were forced to hold a reserve deposit with the Bank of Guatemala equal to 16 percent of their outstanding loans or policy premiums. Interest earned on such reserves was paid at one-half of the current market interest rate. In the case of insurance companies, if premiums were transferred abroad for reinsurance, the income was reported by the insurance company but with no deduction allowed for the cost of the reinsurance. This created problems of double taxation when the premiums associated with reinsurance were taxed abroad as well, and discouraged reinsurance abroad when the domestic reinsurance market was quite thin.

This separate tax regime for financial institutions was largely administered by the regulatory agency, the Superintendent of Banks. This was a convenient administrative arrangement, given the need for specialized expertise and the present understaffing of the Ministry of Finance, but it also created difficulties because of the different objectives of the regulatory and fiscal authorities.

There were serious defects in the Guatemalan regulatory process for financial institutions. One set of problems arose from the poor definition of taxable income. More seriously, the regulatory process repressed the growth of healthy savings institutions, especially by requiring regulated financial institutions to make low-return investments directly or indirectly in central government debt, a process that, as did the required cash reserve ratios on loans and premiums, acted as a hidden tax. The main terms involved requirements that banks keep 41 percent of demand deposits and 13 percent of time deposits in a noninterest-paying reserve with the Bank of Guatemala and that insurance companies keep 40 percent of their reserves in government bonds paying 8 percent nominal interest. A regulation with similar effects was the ceiling on life insurance policy loan interest at 6.5 percent. At prevailing interest rates, the combined effect of these provisions on the gross incomes of banks and insurance companies, was larger than their before-tax income.

The rules specified by the regulatory agency to calculate taxable income tended to understate net income by not requiring full accrual of income and by allowing a bad debt reserve for loans. This understatement was partly offset by regulations that delayed loss recognition. The life insurance regulatory system also understated income of the companies by requiring a low interest rate on reserves, but then the system almost justified itself by forcing the companies, as we have seen, to realize very low returns on the investment of their reserve funds. In life insurance the regulatory system had to come to grips with the development of a more up-to-date life policy form adaptable to an economy with large interest rate fluctuations.

The options for reform in the taxation of financial institutions hinged upon the reform options for the entire corporate income tax. If Guatemala moved to tax total shareholder income, including all interest income, it would be unnecessary to continue to impose a special tax on financial institutions. Banks, insurance companies, and other financial intermediaries would become subject to the general rules of company income taxation. A more controversial issue was whether the tax rate for financial institutions should be somewhat lower than the general rate because of hidden taxes and the much stricter enforcement for financial institutions than for other taxpayers. All in all, the preferred option would have been to incorporate financial institutions in the general regime and to get rid of special hidden taxes. In terms of enforcement, the administrative arrangement through the Superintendent of Banks should probably have continued at least until the Ministry's audit function became better staffed.

Other issues concerning the tax treatment of financial institutions and insurance companies included the treatment of reinsurance, accounting methods, and whole-life insurance. With respect to the tax treatment of reinsurance premiums for insurance companies, the most appropriate approach was to start allowing insurance companies to deduct premiums arising from reinsurance of their policies with foreign companies. To deter strategies geared to eliminate Guatemalan tax through reinsurance schemes with foreign companies, the government considered the option of imposing a substantial withholding tax on the estimated profit associated with reinsurance premiums. In terms of accounting methods, particularly the pre-reform use by financial and insurance institutions of cash accounting for revenues and accrual accounting for expenses, several options were considered to harmonize both sides of the income statement.[15]

Guatemalan tax law should also enable individuals to save through whole-life insurance policies. Pre-reform, benefits paid to the contributor prior to death were fully taxed (with no deduction allowed for premiums). This was a punitive tax treatment of savings carried out through insurance policies. This situation had to be addressed. The simplest approach was to treat insurance savings the same as other tax-assisted savings instruments used for retirement.

There was also a need to revise several rules in the income tax law for the treatment of insurance products. These were the deduction for term insurance premiums in the personal income tax and the different treatment of the pre-death liquidation of a life insurance policy, depending on whether it has been held for longer or less than 10 years. The options for reform included the repeal of the former and the conversion to a single rule for all pre-death liquidations, treating the proceeds as the sale of an asset.

On a different but related area, the annuity (pension) rule in the personal income tax was overly generous (money put aside for pensions was not taxed and the pension income was not taxed) either. However, a strong pension institution did not develop in Guatemala. Such an institution would have been invaluable for social welfare purposes and the development of capital markets. But few other options were available via tax policy to attempt to stimulate the growth of a pension institution. A substantial contribution to capital formation through savings accumulated in pension plans would also have been a boon for the country. However, some time in the future, after pension institutions are developed, the personal income tax law should be amended to tax pension income to the extent that it exceeds tax-paid contributions by the recipient.

Tax Rates

Under the pre-reform corporate income tax, the progressive tax rate schedule was applied to the entire taxable income of a company in a particular net income bracket. Of course, this created notches in which the tax became confiscatory of additional net income. Moreover, there were no provisions for smoothing income over time when companies jumped from one category to another. This penalized enterprises in riskier and more volatile activities. Investments by growing firms were also discouraged by the progressive tax rate structure and its application.

In addition to these perverse incentive effects, the progressive rate structure may have encouraged taxpayers to organize activities into separate smaller companies to take advantage of the lower rates. However, the pre-reform low-tax-rate brackets used for company tax purposes involved relatively small amounts of income (up to Q60,000), thereby mitigating the impact on the breakup of companies.

Multiple tax rates may also have encouraged related companies to undertake transactions, especially of a financial nature, to minimize company taxes. A company facing a low tax rate may issue equity rather than debt to a company facing a high tax rate. Since intercorporate dividends were tax-free, the effect of a financial transaction of this sort would be to transfer interest deductions from low- to high-tax-rate companies.

All these considerations led to the conclusion that it would be more desirable to use a single rate for company income taxation. If the personal income tax has a progressive rate schedule, the single rate for the company tax should be equal to the maximum personal rate. This would facilitate the (partial) integration of the personal and corporate income taxes.

Additional Measures to Improve Enforcement

Almost two-thirds of companies in Guatemala paid little or no company tax pre-reform. In part, this was a reflection of a poorly designed tax base that allowed much income to escape taxation. However, there was also ample evidence that the small number of companies with a positive tax liability was purely and simply due to tax evasion. The government of Guatemala considered two sets of options for helping to enforce the company income tax. The first was to develop a set of withholding taxes on capital income as a backstop to the company income tax system. The second was to levy a general minimum tax.[16]

Withholding Taxes on Income Accruing to Residents

To enforce the company income tax, authorities considered expanding the use of withholding taxes on income paid by companies to residents in Guatemala. Pre-reform, Guatemala imposed withholding taxes on qualifying interest paid to residents and on dividends, branch profits, interest, and other income remitted to nonresidents. To ensure the taxation of income earned by investors, withholding taxes were applied to all remitted income. The withholding tax was credited by taxpayers against the income tax payable on the specified income. On interest income and other forms of deductible expenses (fees and commissions) at the company level, a withholding tax, say at the rate of 15 percent, could be assessed (increased from 4 percent) and made creditable against personal income taxes. Companies receiving interest, fees, and similar income from other companies could credit withholding taxes against company taxes they owed on such income.

If dividend income were kept exempt at the personal level to avoid double taxation of dividend income, a withholding tax on dividends could be used, making it creditable against company income taxes to avoid double taxation of dividend income. The dividend withholding tax acted as a minimum tax on distributed company income. This arrangement has been used in other countries but it is not free of complications.

A General Minimum Tax

Another method of enforcing the company income tax was to consider a general minimum tax applicable to all companies operating in Guatemala. A minimum tax has two particular advantages. First, the tax ensures fairness which improves the willingness of companies to comply, since all companies pay some tax. Second, the tax may allow the government to reduce the value of certain tax incentives that are otherwise politically difficult to abolish.

A minimum tax also has disadvantages, such as the treatment of companies that face fluctuating income or uneven growth and those that may be in a loss position. The minimum tax also complicates tax administration and compliance. There are several types of minimum taxes used throughout the world. Alternative taxes on assets or net worth have become more popular around the world over the last decade.[17] Some European countries have such a tax. Germany levies a net assets tax with a rate between 0.6 and 0.75 percent, and this tax is not allowed as a deduction or a credit from the regular corporate income tax. Austria has a net assets tax with a rate of 1.35 percent, but this tax is allowed as a deduction from the regular corporate income tax. Norway uses a 0.3 percent tax on net assets, and no deduction is allowed from the corporate income tax. In the United States, several states have net worth taxes and also alternative minimum franchise taxes. The United States government imposes an alternative minimum tax, but this tax falls on income (20 percent on the regular net income base grossed up for tax preferences) rather than on assets.

Business taxes on assets have become particularly popular in Latin America.[18] Mexico implemented an alternative asset tax 5 years ago, and since then many other countries in Latin America, such as Argentina and Venezuela, have introduced some form of business asset tax. In Latin America, in particular, taxes of this type are actually used as administrative measures for controlling evasion when the tax administration apparatus cannot make the corporate income tax work properly. Business taxes on assets are used as a method of presumptive income taxation, based on the idea that capital assets will produce some minimum rate of return on average, or otherwise the enterprise will get out of the business. For this reason, asset taxes are almost always used as alternative minimum taxes creditable against the regular corporate income tax, and often they can be carried forward as a credit for several years. But allowing the asset tax to be carried forward as a credit still does not solve the problem that the tax imposes a burden when a firm can least afford it. Actually, the credit provides relief when the firm is in a better position and may not need the relief. The option seriously considered by the government was a capital asset tax (similar to the minor "annual quota tax" in force in Guatemala) that would be applied to the gross assets of the company and would work as a creditable minimum tax. The distinct advantage of this tax for Guatemala was that enforcement would not rely on the reporting of income, and thus might be more difficult to evade. However, the distinct disadvantage of this tax—that it is payable even if the company is incurring true economic losses—weighed heavily in the argument for relatively low rates.

Company Tax Incentives

In the pre-reform tax regime, the system of fiscal incentives for corporations in Guatemala had two main components: factor-based incentives (investment and employment) and sector-based incentives, including substantial incentives on nontraditional exports.[19]

The factor-based incentives were contained in the pre-reform income tax law and provided the following incentives for investment and employment:

- Investment incentive in the form of an additional deduction from taxable income of 10 percent (20 percent for businesses with less than Q200,000 in assets) of the value of new machinery and equipment. To qualify for the benefit, the machinery and equipment had to be used in the production process of the business and installed and in use for at least nine months of the tax year. Because of the graduated tax-rate schedules, this incentive was equivalent to an investment tax credit (ITC) of between 1.2 percent and 6.8 percent, depending on the tax bracket of the company.
- Employment incentive in the form of a tax credit equivalent to the contributions paid by employers to social security (I.G.S.S.) for the increment from the previous year, in the number of employees earning less than Q500 a month. The credit was equal to 50 percent of the annual increment in employers' social

security contributions for businesses established in the department of Guatemala and 100 percent for businesses operating
outside the capital. The equivalent maximum credit per additional employee therefore was Q30 for businesses in Guatemala and
Q36 for businesses outside Guatemala.

The sector-based incentives were granted by law on an individual
basis—by economic sector—and included agricultural, industrial, and
export activities. Among the agricultural incentives, were poultry, rubber,
rabbit, and milk production promotion laws. The reforestation law
provided a tax credit for taxpayers who incurred expenses for the
reforestation of areas of at least 5 hectares. The credit was equal to the
cost of planting new trees and maintenance of the reforested area and
was limited to 50 percent of the firm's tax liability. Over the last four
decades, Guatemala enacted several different industrial incentive laws in
an effort to diversify the economy and reduce its dependence on
traditional agricultural exports.

In 1979, the National Congress enacted the Ley de Fomento para
Descentralización Industrial (Law 29-79, Industrial Decentralization
Promotion Law), to promote industrial investment in areas other than the
department of Guatemala. Under this law, new firms could receive a
partial business income tax exemption (between 70 percent and 90
percent) for 8 to 10 years depending on the area where the business was
established. The country was divided into four main regions, with the
region farthest from the capital receiving the most generous exemptions.
In addition, this law allowed businesses already established outside the
department of Guatemala to qualify for benefits. These firms were
allowed to *deduct* from their taxable income their investment for a given
tax period as long as the investment resulted in an increase of at least 10
percent of total assets from the previous year.

The Decentralization Law also offered similar incentives to small
businesses. Small businesses are defined as those with fewer than thirty
workers and whose machinery, equipment, and tools do not exceed a
value of Q50,000. The benefits to small business also varied with location.
Depending on location, benefits included exemption from 60 percent to
100 percent of import duties on machinery, equipment, spare parts, and
raw materials for a period ranging between 8 and 10 years. It also
granted exemption from income taxes ranging from 80 percent to 100
percent, for up to 10 years.

Other industrial incentive laws under the pre-reform regime included
mining, renewable sources of energy, books, newspapers, and the rest of

the media. The tourism industry also benefited from incentive laws that provided

- a one-time exemption from customs duties on all construction materials, furniture, equipment, and appliances.
- exemption from local tax on new construction or expansion.
- a 100 percent exemption from income tax for new construction, for five years, and a 50 percent exemption from income tax for the five subsequent years.
- a 100 percent exemption from tax for additions or renovations of existing structures for two-and-one-half years, and a 50 percent exemption from tax for the subsequent two and one-half years on income attributable to the addition or remodeling.
- a 100 percent income tax exemption for ten years for enterprises with more than 50 percent of their capital from Guatemalan sources or enterprises that established hotels in areas with no other tourist establishment.

Tax incentives were also provided to promote exports. In 1989, the National Congress enacted a new Free Trade Zone Law, containing three main sets of provisions. First, free trade zones could be established anywhere in the country (with the approval of the Ministry of the Economy) and were administered by private investors. The administrators of the zones enjoyed a 15-year exemption on the income from the trade zone. They also benefited from an exemption from customs duties on any imported materials and machinery necessary to construct the trade zone infrastructure or necessary for its operation, an exemption from stamp tax on sale of trade zone property to its tenants, and a five-year exemption from property tax. Second, service, industrial, and commercial establishments operating in the trade zones were exempted from VAT on sales within the zone or between two trade zones and total exemption from income taxes on income generated in the trade zone. The income tax exemption was granted for 12 years for service and industrial establishments and 5 years for commercial establishments. Machinery, equipment, tools, and raw materials were exempt from customs duties. Businesses established in free trade zones were allowed to sell up to 20 percent of their output to the domestic market. The law also allowed businesses benefiting from other export incentive legislation to apply for free trade zone status. If granted, the accumulated years of exemptions under the export incentive legislation would be deducted from the period of exemption under the Free Trade Zone Law.

In addition, a new export promotion law was introduced in June of

1990. This law distinguished among four different types of exporting businesses, each enjoying different forms of incentives:

- *Temporary Admission Regime*: Provided suspension of customs duties and value-added tax (VAT) to raw materials, product samples, and intermediate inputs used in the production or assembly of goods for export outside the Central America Common Market (CACM).
- *Reimbursement of Duties Regime*: Provided reimbursement of customs duties and VAT for businesses that produce goods for export using imports that originally paid these taxes. These businesses also enjoyed income tax exemption on profits from exports and exemption from export taxes but did not receive exemption of customs duties and VAT on machinery and equipment.
- *Export of Full Domestic Value-Added Regime*: Businesses producing goods for exports with no imported components enjoyed tax exemption for up to 10 years on income from exports and from customs duties and VAT on imported machinery and equipment used in the production of exports.
- *Custom Duties Credit Regime*: This regime affected "indirect exporters." If a local business sold a product used as an input in the production of a good for export, the local business received a customs duties credit equal to the duties paid on the input used in the export. This credit could be used to offset duties on subsequent imports of raw material and intermediate goods.

This maze of tax incentives and tax holidays available to Guatemalan companies created significant difficulties for authorities in charge of administering the company tax. One problem common to most of Guatemala's incentives was the frequent opportunity for manipulation of transactions between exempt and non-exempt firms. The potential implications of this behavior were especially acute in Guatemala because corporations were not required to consolidate their activities for tax purposes. Firms with the same owners were always allowed to file separate returns, making it easier for taxpayers to engage in artificial transfer pricing of goods and services. The problem was also compounded because almost all companies in Guatemala are privately held and a significant portion of these issue bearer stock. It was therefore nearly impossible for tax inspectors to identify the stockholders of related companies. Tax administration practices made things more difficult. In practice the auditors did not audit companies that qualified for tax incentives because the examination of a company not paying tax was perceived to have little or no value for enforcement and revenue collections.

The economic effects of fiscal incentives are in general very difficult to measure because the necessary data are rarely available. The case of Guatemala was no exception. There had been very little information or systematic research on the effect of the various incentives on economic activity. From the benefits side, the relevant issue was how much higher output and employment were compared to the situation in which the incentives did not exist. Here only rough estimates could be obtained. The data suggested that the export incentive law may have contributed to a net increase in economic activity in the food and apparel industry. However, it was not possible to attribute the change in economic activity to the fiscal incentives.

The economic costs of incentive legislation arise from the revenue loss due to reduced tax liability and from increased administrative costs. There are several reasons for the reduction in government tax receipts attributable to tax incentives: the exemption of previously taxable firms, the reduction in taxes due to the competitive displacement of non-exempt firms by exempt firms, and the revenue drain arising from transfer pricing practices. Information on the latter two revenue effects was unavailable.

With respect to the possibility of direct revenue losses, different scenarios could be considered. It could be argued that all of the incentives had been completely effective in the sense that no firm had received a tax break for doing what it would have done anyway in the absence of incentives. On the other hand, there are two quite different sets of circumstances under which the incentives would be totally ineffective and a complete waste of the tax revenue would occur. First, either domestic or foreign firms may receive an inframarginal subsidy that has no influence on their marginal investment decisions. Firms are rewarded without achieving any desired change in their behavior. Second, foreign firms may not benefit from the incentive if the treasury in their home country appropriates its value. Without tax sparing, tax incentives granted for foreign capital in Guatemala may be undone by reduced foreign tax credits allowed for Guatemalan-source income when remitted to the parent. This is particularly important because Guatemala's major source of foreign capital, the United States, does not allow tax incentives to pass through without reducing foreign tax credits for U.S. tax purposes, even in the presence of a treaty.

As a rough order of magnitude, the revenue loss associated with Guatemala's pre-reform incentive program, assuming complete ineffectiveness, was estimated as Q36 million, based on the information from corporate and individual income tax returns in 1989. This represents approximately 9 percent of total personal and company income tax revenue in 1989. In addition to the revenue loss due to the incentives, the government spent additional resources in administration and supervision. The ministry most involved with the incentive legislation is the Ministry of the Economy and, within that ministry, the Industrial Policy Division (PDI). Officials at PDI estimate its incentive-related expenditures for 1990 at about Q800,000.

In addition to these revenue and administrative cost burdens, incentives inflict a social cost on the economy by reducing the efficiency with which resources are allocated. The main economic distortions created by the incentive structure affected intersectoral and intrasectoral resource allocation. In both cases resources were not allocated to those activities with the highest economic return. Adding all three types of costs—revenue, administration, and excess burden costs—it was quite possible that several incentive laws provided a negative value-added to the economy.

One possibility for reform considered was the abolition of all tax incentives used in the pre-reform tax regime for such items as export, industrial, agricultural, regional, and tourist activities. The final decision was made more difficult by the fact that it was not possible to carry out a careful review of the economic net benefits associated with the incentives. These data limitations notwithstanding, the analysis suggested that the export incentive legislation may have provided a net benefit to the Guatemalan economy if at least 25 to 50 percent of all firms enjoying incentives had located in Guatemala in direct response to the incentives. These figures did not include any evasion due to income shifting from taxable to nontaxable firms, nor did they include efficiency costs from intrasectoral resource allocation. All other incentives, it was concluded, were very likely to have produced no net increase in investment.

In light of the suggestive quantitative analysis and the administrative characteristics and capabilities, the option for reform finally considered was the elimination of all tax incentives except for the export-promotion and free trade zone laws. Alternatively, all export-promotion incentives—except for the free trade zones—could be replaced by a deduction equal to a percentage of the value of exported goods as verified by customs.

In consolidating all incentives for export promotion, the reform option included the amendment of the free trade zone law to eliminate access to the domestic market of 20 percent of free trade zone output. This provision, included to make the trade zones more attractive, had only served to displace domestic producers and thus represented a net cost to the economy. That provision also needlessly complicated the administration of the free trade zones. The option for reform also included the transformation of the investment incentive deduction of 10 percent of purchases of new machinery and equipment assets (20 percent for smaller companies) into an investment credit. An investment tax credit equal to a percentage of depreciable investment expenditures could be easily calculated, since the cost of acquired assets is used for depreciation purposes. Also, the credit had a lower revenue cost to the government compared to a tax holiday because only new investment projects were subsidized. A credit is of the same value to companies no matter what their tax rate. And, the credit could be better controlled by requiring companies to obtain a certificate from authorities.

Proposed and Actual Reforms

The Project finally recommended a sweeping reform of the structure of business income taxes. Most of the recommendations were accepted by the Guatemalan government and were enacted for the tax year 1993. The following are the Project's major proposals for reform of company taxation and a description of the reforms were finally enacted by the government in the Guatemalan Tax Modernization Program of 1992.

- Adopt either a simple flat rate of 30 percent or a general rate of 34 percent together with a lower rate of 18 percent for companies with earnings under Q50,000. The government adopted a 25 percent flat rate tax. This was consistent with the recommendation of the Project that the company tax rate and the top individual tax rate be the same. The 25 percent flat rate chosen by the government was lower than would be consistent with revenue neutrality.
- Adopt a residence-based method of taxing foreign-source income. This proposal was not adopted.
- Fully tax interest income and fully deduct of interest costs. The government accepted this recommendation. A problem is created however, because interest income to individuals is taxed at only 10 percent, while the value of the deduction under the business tax is 25 percent of taxable income. Still, this is a better situation than under the previous law where there was deductibility at 34 percent but not taxation of interest income.
- Retain exemption of company dividends and capital gains at the personal level as the method of integration of corporate and personal income taxes. This recommendation of the Project was partially accepted. The income tax became partly integrated because the top personal rate is 25 percent and there is no

adjustment for individuals who are in a lower bracket. Capital gains became taxed under the new income tax at a 15 percent final tax rate.

- Allow full deduction of fringe benefits for employees but include them in taxable personal income. The government rejected this recommendation. The government, however, introduced more stringent limitations to curb abuses, e.g., the deductibility of fringes was limited to employees, and excluded fringes given to families of employees.

- Include capital gains in company taxable income without three-year installments and without revaluation adjustment. Index capital gains for inflation only if there is full indexation of the income tax. The government did eliminate the three-year installment feature. A new revaluation tax was introduced which partially eliminates the objections to the revaluation of assets. The government chose not to adopt indexation.

- Allow company losses to be carried forward for three years for tax purposes. The government decided on a four-year carryforward.

- Adopt a "pooled class" concept for depreciation allowances using a declining balance method and index depreciation allowances for inflation only with full indexation of the tax. The government decided to make no change in the depreciation schedule.

- Leave in place the present system of inventory valuation. If full indexation for inflation is adopted, then switch to a FIFO method. There was no change in the method of inventory valuation.

- Replace the pre-reform 2 percent bad debt deduction with a method based on actual experience. The government decided to increase the bad debt deduction to 3 percent.

- Retain the pre-reform withholding rate at 12.5 percent for dividends paid to foreigners. Lower the withholding rate for interest and other income paid to foreigners to 20 percent. The government adopted a program more or less consistent with the recommendation of the project. The new withholding rates on foreigners became

> 12.5 percent on dividends and interest.
> 25.0 percent on royalties.
> 12.5 percent on all else.

- Eliminate all tax incentives except for the two export promotion laws. These two laws could be phased out at a later date, keeping only the Free Trade Zone incentives. The government did eliminate most of the incentive programs, other than those for export promotion, but "grandfathered" benefits granted under a predetermined period. The new income tax law also allows for an additional 25 percent deduction from taxable income of the reinvested profits during the period.

- Tax financial institutions under the general company tax regime at regular rates. Government should pay market rates to financial institutions for their investments in government bonds. The government adopted the taxation of all financial institutions at the regular rate of 25 percent. However, foreign domiciled insurance companies pay a 10 percent tax on all premium gross income. This latter measure may be prudent until tax administration capabilities are further developed. Changes in regulatory requirements were postponed.

- Make insurance companies use full accrual accounting and "actual experience" provisions for bad debt reserves. Allow insurance companies a full deduction for reinsurance premiums, but introduce a withholding tax on these payments. Give the savings component of whole life insurance policies the same treatment given to pension funds. Repeal the personal deduction for life insurance premiums and tax pre-death liquidations of life insurance policies as the sale of an asset. No changes were made to the way financial institutions, including insurance companies, calculate their reserves.

- Disallow the present advantage for long-term contracts (timing of cost deductions and recognizing income) by using a "completed contract" method or by capitalizing costs to the time income is earned or the asset is sold. The provisions in the previous law were not changed.

- Extend the method for depletion deduction currently granted to forestry companies to mining and petroleum companies for the capitalized value of exploration and development expenses. The provisions in the previous law were not changed.

- Expand the withholding tax to all remitted income (other than dividends) within Guatemala at a rate of 15 percent and make it creditable against personal income taxes. The government introduced a withholding final tax on interest income at a rate of 10 percent. Transport companies not domiciled by Guatemala pay a 3 percent tax of gross revenues as a definitive tax. Cinematographic and news companies pay a 60 percent rate on gross revenues as a definitive tax. No withholding measures for other sources of nonwage income were introduced.

- Consider the introduction of a general minimum tax based on net worth at a rate of 2 percent and make it creditable against company income tax. The government did not adopt a minimum tax. Instead, it opted to strengthen the method of calculating quarterly advance payments. For most companies and self-employed individuals, the quarterly installments are 1.5 percent of gross sales. For selected other special cases and for firms with gross sales less than Q600,000, the rate is 1 percent. The government felt these measures would act as a minimum tax, in part because the claim for a refund will require an audit and most firms will not want to submit to that.

- If high inflation rates persist in Guatemala, consider full indexation of the income tax. Inflation has moderated, and the government opted for no indexation.

Impact of the Tax Reforms

To recapitulate, the major reforms for the company tax adopted by the government in the Tax Modernization Program included the adoption of a flat 25 percent rate, the taxation of previously exempt interest income at a flat rate of 10 percent, the taxation of capital gains at 15 percent, the taxation of financial institutions at the regular rate of 25 percent, the increase in the reserve for bad debts from 2 percent to 3 percent, the introduction of a deduction for 25 percent of reinvested profits, and the elimination of many fiscal incentives and tax holiday provisions.

The impact of the tax reforms includes not only the implications of the new measures, but also the substitution or elimination of old ones.[20] The tax expenditures related to the special provisions and incentives for business income existing in 1992 prior to the reform are summarized in Table 3.6. As can be seen, only a few provisions had a significant impact, as measured by either the number of firms, the percent of taxpayers affected, or the impact on tax liabilities. Many of the fiscal incentives in the pre-reform tax law were quite insignificant.[21] The most significant incentives in terms of revenue cost were the Reforestation Credit (Q4.6 million), the Industrial Export Incentive Credit (Q10.4 million), and the Industrial Decentralization Credit (Q43 million). The tax expenditures related to the special treatment of certain types of income under the pre-reform corporate income tax are also presented in Table 3.6. The exemption from income tax of all interest income alone represented a foregone revenue for government in 1992 of Q51 million. The tax reform eliminated all the special provisions listed in Table 3.6 with the exception of the provisions related to export promotion.

The overall simulation results for the revenue impact of the reform in the business income tax are presented in Table 6.1. In comparison to the projections for the baseline case, the tax reform program increases fiscal revenues from businesses for 1992 and 1993, but it results in lower revenues for 1994. The flat income tax rate for business income decreases the elasticity of the business income tax toward 1 in 1994, as corresponds to a flat rate tax.

The changes in tax collections from the most important changes in business income taxation are presented in Table 6.2. It is clear from this table that the most costly provision of the reform was the introduction of a flat rate at 25 percent. This would cost Q179 million in foregone revenue in 1994. The second most important provision in terms of foregone revenues was the deduction for reinvested profits, decreasing tax accruals by Q80 million in 1994. In the long run, the business income tax reform would be a net revenue loser.

TABLE 6.1: Business Income Tax Reform: Estimated Impacts

1. Revenue Impact

	(Fiscal Years, Q million)		
	1992	*1993*	*1994*
Baseline Projection	Q816	Q 937	Q1,084
Tax Modernization Program	839	1,098	873
Difference	23	161	-209
Tax Liability GDP Elasticity			
Baseline Projection	NA	1.09	1.13
Tax Modernization Program	NA	NA	1.02

2. Tax Burden Impact (1992)

Household Income Class	*Baseline*		*Tax Modernization Program*	
	Number of Households (thousands)	*Effective Tax Burden*	*Effective Tax Burden*	*Difference in Effective Tax Burden*
Under Q2,465	180.9	1.8	1.4	-0.4
Q2,465 - 3,750	182.2	1.7	1.3	-0.4
Q3,750 - 5,250	181.5	1.6	1.2	-0.4
Q5,250 - 7,250	182.4	1.5	1.1	-0.4
Q7,250 - 9,450	181.3	1.1	0.9	-0.2
Q9,450 - 12,700	182.9	1.4	1.1	-0.3
Q12,700 - 17,600	182.4	1.2	0.9	-0.3
Q17,600 - 25,550	181.3	1.2	0.9	-0.3
Q25,550 - 43,250	181.5	0.9	0.7	-0.2
Q43,250 and Over	183.4	1.9	1.4	-0.5
Q43,250 - 74,450	93.3	0.6	0.5	-0.1
Q74,450 - 230,000	71.6	1.5	1.2	-0.3
Over Q230,000	18.5	2.8	2.2	-0.6
Total	1,819.7	1.6	1.2	-0.4

(continued)

TABLE 6.1 (cont.): Business Income Tax Reform: Estimated Impacts

3. Impact by Type of Company (1992):

(a) Standard Industry Classification	Number of Firms	Baseline Tax Liability	Simulation Tax Liability	Difference	Percent Change in Tax Liability
Agriculture, Forestry, Hunting, Fishing	995	Q37,373	Q21,566	Q-15,807	-42.3%
Mining & Quarrying	62	11,058	5,138	-5,920	-53.5
Manufacturing Industries	2,211	199,633	116,094	-83,538	-41.8
Electricity, Gas & Water	30	24,920	14,043	-10,877	-43.6
Construction	570	10,870	6,141	-4,729	-43.5
Commerce-Wholesale, Retail;Restaurant, Hotel	4,667	196,088	115,347	-80,740	-41.2
Transportation, Storage and Communication	474	25,222	13,282	-11,940	-47.3
Finance and Insurance Services	2,359	44,393	26,892	-17,500	-39.4
Community, Social and Personal Services	1,514	19,134	11,429	-7,705	-40.3
Not Able to Classify	2,133	16,764	10,987	-5,776	-34.5
Total	15,019	Q585,461	Q340,924	Q-244,536	-41.8%

(b) Asset Size Classification (Q thousands)

			Number of Firms	Baseline	Simulation	Difference	Percent Change
Q0	<	50	2,799	Q2,140	Q2,013	Q-126	-5.9%
50	<	200	2,787	10,420	7,894	-2,525	-24.2
200	<	500	2,594	20,864	14,148	-6,715	-32.2
500	<	2,500	4,265	96,226	58,437	-37,789	-39.3
2,500	<	5,000	1,337	72,388	41,494	-30,894	-42.7
5,000	<	20,000	900	163,367	92,315	-71,052	-43.5
20,000	<	100,000	287	184,869	105,096	-79,773	-43.2
100,000	<	******	47	35,183	19,524	-15,659	-44.5
Total			15,019	Q585,461	Q340,924	Q-244,536	-41.8%

NOTE: Does not include regulated financial institutions or taxes paid through definitive withholding taxes.

Source: Ministry of Finance, Government of Guatemala, as reported to *Consultoria Para La Administracion Fiscal*, Policy Economics Group, KPMG Peat Marwick, and Policy Research Program, Georgia State University, 1991-1993.

TABLE 6.2: Business Income Tax Reforms: Revenue Implications

	Revenue Effect (FY 94)	
	Amount (Millions of Quetzales)	Percent of Baseline Revenue
25% tax rate	-Q179	-16.5%
NOLs allowed up to 4 years	*	*
Depreciation - Office equipment	-7	-0.0
Bad Debts Reserve Deduction	-9	-0.0
Reinvestment deduction - 20%	-80	-0.1
Transportation companies presumptive income	-2	-0.0
International news presumptive income	†	†
Travel expenses (limited to 5% of gross income)	-2	-0.0
Mining exploration costs (amortization - 1 or 5 yrs.)	-2	-0.0
Gross sales tax (max tax: 1% of gross sales)	-26	-0.0
Investment incentive (repeal)	1	0.0
Employment incentive (repeal)	†	†
Education incentive (repeal)	†	†
Financial institutions (25% rate)	7	0.0
Capital gains - 15% separate rate	4	0.0
Quota annual (0.1% net assets capped at Q20 million)	2	0.0
Reevaluation of assets	35	0.0
Interest income (10% withholding rate)	34	0.0
Gross sales tax estimated payments	13	0.0
Total	-210	-19.4

*Less than Q1 million, less than 0.01 percent; †Less than Q500,000, less than 0.01 percent.
Source: Ministry of Finance, Government of Guatemala, as reported to *Consultoria Para la Administracion Fiscal*, Policy Economics Group, KPMG Peat Marwick, and Policy Research Program, Georgia State University, 1991-1993.

The impact of the reform on the distribution of tax burdens is presented also in Table 6.1. This table compares the distribution of effective tax rates by household income class under the pre-reform system with the new tax introduced in the Tax Modernization Program. The tax burden impacts for both the pre-reform and the reformed tax are computed under the assumption that 50 percent of the tax burden is shifted back to all capital owners, and the remaining 50 percent is shifted back to workers in the form of lower wages. (This is a compromise assumption. The question of the incidence of corporate income taxes is far from being resolved in the public finance literature. Depending on factor mobility, elasticities of demand and supply, market conditions, and other economic parameters, owners of a firm, all capital owners in the country, owners of other inputs of production such as land and labor, and even the consumer of goods and services produced by a firm, may all bear, in varying proportions, the burden of the business income tax.)[22]

The overall tax burden from the business income tax falls from 1.6 percent of household income for the pre-reform tax to 1.2 percent for the new tax in the Tax Modernization Program. By income group, the reduction in effective tax burdens is larger at the bottom and top of the income distribution. This is again a reflection of the incidence assumption that the burden of the business income tax is borne in equal proportions by workers and all capital owners.

The impact on the different sectors of the economy of the changes in business income taxation in the Tax Modernization Program is presented in the last part of Table 6.1. This table also presents the impact of the changes by asset size of the firms. The overall reduction in business income tax liabilities of 41.8 percent is distributed quite evenly across the different sectors of the economy. The highest reduction in tax liability is for the Mining and Quarrying sector, 53.5 percent, and the lowest reduction is for the Finance and Insurance Services sector, with a reduction of 39.4 percent. In the case of asset size, the reduction in tax liability increases steadily with the firm's asset size from a reduction of 24.2 percent for firms with assets under Q200,000 to a reduction of 44.5 percent for firms with assets over Q100 million. The smallest firms, those with assets under Q50,000, pay little business tax to begin with, and they experience a decrease in tax liability of only 5.9 percent.

One main objective of the company tax reform was to make the company tax a less distortionary method of withholding shareholder income. The elimination of some of the distortions in timing, valuation, and incentive issues should help reduce the distortions among economic sectors identified in the computation of the METRs. Still, without full indexation of the income tax, some distortion will exist and its level will increase with the inflation rate. The value of the company income tax reform will be the increased efficiency (or potential GDP) that will accompany the elimination of distortions in the allocation of resources. Unfortunately, welfare impact of these changes cannot be measured here.

Notes

1.   This chapter draws on a number of technical memoranda: McLure (1989), Mintz (1991), Thuronyi (1990), Brannon (1990), Mutti (1991), Zodrow (1990), and Ramos and Thirsk (1991).

2.   A cash method of accounting was also allowed for taxpayers not required to maintain books of accounts and for all types of agricultural firms.

3.   For further discussions of many of the issues raised in this section, see Boadway, Bruce, and Mintz (1982, 1987), Royal Commission of Taxation (1966), and Meade (1978).

4.   For a full discussion of the concept and computation of METRs, see Auerbach (1984), Boadway (1988), Bradford and Fullerton (1981), and King and Fullerton (1984).

5.   See McLure (1989).

6.   See for example Meade (1978); Bradford (1986);   McLure, Mutti, Thuronyi, and Zodrow (1989); McLure and Zodrow (forthcoming).

7.   For the importance of integration issues in developing countries, see Harberger (1990).

8.   Incentives are discussed more fully in the section on Company Tax Incentives, later in this chapter.

9.   See Rajaram (1989).

10.   See Mintz (1991) and Rajaram (1989).

11.   See Frenkel, Razim and Sadka (1991) and Mutti (1991).

12.   Yet, the previous history of large negative real rates of return earned on bank deposits in Guatemala and the absence of large outflows of capital abroad suggested that this condition of substitutability between domestic and foreign investments did not strongly hold.

13.   For a further discussion of the issues discussed in this section, see Ballentine and McLure (1980); Galper, Lucke and Toder (1988); Harberger (1990); Hines and Hubbard (1990); Leechor and Mintz (1990); and Shah and Slemrod (1990).

14.   This section draws heavily on Brannon (1990). For further discussion of the issues discussed in this section, see also Barham, Poddar and Whalley (1987); Biderman and Tucillo (1976); Hoffman, Poddar and Whalley (1987); McLure, Mutti, Thuronyi and Zodrow (1989); and Martinez-Vazquez (1989).

15.   See Brannon (1990).

16.   For a general discussion of tax administration and tax reform issues with emphasis in Latin American countries, see Bird and Casanegra (1992).

17. See Estache (1990).

18. See Byrne (1994).

19. This section draws heavily on Ramos and Thirsk (1991) and Mintz (1991). See also Bird (1980), Harberger (1981), Mintz (1988), Shah and Toye (1978), Thirsk (1985), and Usher (1977).

20. This section draws heavily on Galper and Ramos (1992).

21. See Ramos and Thirsk (1991).

22. See, for example, Harberger (1962), Mieszkowski (1969), Newberry and Stern (1987), Shah and Whalley (1990), and Wasylenko (1991).

7

Value-Added Tax and Other Taxes: Proposals and Reform

The pre-reform 7 percent value-added tax (VAT) was applied to sales at importation and to domestic sales of taxable goods, at the wholesale and retail distribution level.[1] Non-personal services were also subject to the pre-reform VAT. The basic legal structure of the tax was sound because it had a single rate,[2] but exempt and zero-rated goods did narrow the base significantly. The basic problem in Guatemala was that the VAT had a low rate, several important items were excluded from the base, and enforcement was weak. The result was an inadequate revenue yield, horizontal inequities, widespread evasion, and a lack of confidence in the tax. Clearly, any structural reform would have to be supported by a significant improvement in the tax administration. In terms of policy, the government had to face up to the choice between keeping the nominal rate low and broadening the base by eliminating many of the present exclusions. Ultimately, it chose the former.

The Pre-Reform VAT System

The value-added tax has been the mainstay of the Guatemalan system, accounting for about one-third of revenues. Guatemala's reliance on the VAT has been heavy by comparison to other Latin American countries (only Chile shows a heavier reliance on this tax). However, as a percent of total indirect tax revenues, Guatemala's VAT share has remained relatively low by international standards, reflecting the low rate, the exclusions from the base, and the still significant role played by the stamp tax. Revenue growth has been strong. VAT collections increased steadily from Q142.5 million in 1984 (the first full year of operation) to

Q781.2 million in 1990, i.e., from 1.5 percent of GDP in 1984 to 2.3 percent in 1990.

Because of exemptions, zero-rating, and outright evasion, the tax did not reach its revenue potential. By comparison to the statutory rate of 7 percent, the effective rate on domestic value-added tax was 1.4 percent (Table 2.5), and that on imports was 5.3 percent (Table 2.6). Second, there was a deterioration in the revenue performance of the tax, and the income elasticity had fallen off to less than unity in 1989 and 1990 (Table 2.1). Moreover, flaws in the structure and administration of the tax brought about undesirable equity effects and compromised the efficiency of the Guatemalan economy.

Tax Rate

By international standards, there was ample room for Guatemala to increase its use of the value-added tax. The 7-percent rate was quite low by world standards; 10 percent is a more common figure, and rates as high as 20 percent are not uncommon. Value-Added tax rates for Latin American countries are shown in Table 7.1. The Guatemalan rate is one of the lowest. If competitive pressures were to be a constraint to reform, there would be no problem with Guatemala increasing its tax rate.

The major constraint to increasing the tax rate was political. It was feared that a higher rate would be seen as a surrender to higher taxes and more government, a particularly abhorrent prospect in Guatemala. In fact, a 10 percent rate (suggested by numerous analysts to lessen the deficit and provide money for refunds) was enacted in 1983 but pushed back to 7 percent after a few months.

The Threshold for Registration

Sellers of commodities or services with gross taxable sales under Q12,000 annually, or having less than three employees (five for services), were defined as below the threshold under the pre-reform VAT. This sales figure, equivalent to less than US $2,500 per year, also was low by international standards. The use of the joint criterion of sales volume and number of employees, although not unique to Guatemala, is not commonly used.[3] The use of the number of employees as a criterion has the great advantage of being relatively easy to administer but the disadvantage of possibly discouraging employment.[4]

How should the level of sales volume for VAT coverage be determined? There is no precise answer to this question, and there is considerable variety in the practice. If the objective is to minimize administration burdens without sacrificing significant amounts of tax

TABLE 7.1: Basic VAT Rates in Selected Latin American Countries: 1991

Country	Percentage
Argentina	16%
Bolivia[a]	11
Brazil[b]	11, 17
Chile	18
Columbia	10
Costa Rica	8
Dominican Republic	6
Ecuador	6
Guatemala	**7**
Haiti	10
Honduras	7
Mexico	15
Nicaragua	10
Panama	5
Paraguay	12
Peru	18
Trinidad and Tobago	15
Uruguay	22

[a]Effective rate.
[b]The lower rate is on intrastate transactions.
Source: Tait (1991) pp. 2-3.

revenues, a relatively high threshold should be chosen. There is no hard and fast rule here; Japan offers complete exemption from VAT for firms with up to $200,000 in turnover, whereas Denmark exempts only those whose turnover is less than $1,500.

In Guatemala, the pre-reform threshold applied to firms that were not likely to keep adequate records, i.e., where the government was unable to effectively enforce compliance. By comparison with other developing countries, the Guatemalan threshold was low, and many small traders were theoretically in the net. However, while many small firms were registered, there was evidence that a large number that were legally required to register did not do so. If all the latter were registered, the effect on administration would have been overwhelming. In fact, the pre-reform floor for registration was low enough that significant administrative effort was expended for relatively little revenue return. Of 21,000 firms registered for the VAT, the 13,749 smallest firms contributed only Q7 million in revenues, i.e., only 3.6 percent of collections. The administrative gains from raising the threshold were apparent.

The arguments against raising the threshold were that an unfair advantage would be given to small traders, and that some traders might be induced to split their business in order to take advantage of the registration rule. There were also political problems. Tait (1991, pp. 14-15) points out that much of the opposition to Korea's VAT came from small businesses.

If it were to be decided that the administrative advantages of a higher threshold outweighed the disadvantages, then the question became how high to set the threshold. There is no set rule, and the best choice will vary from country to country. One acceptable criteria is to choose that level at which it is expected that firms will carry out effective recordkeeping.

An important issue related to the registration threshold is that of voluntary registration. Most countries allow for voluntary registration of firms that are under the threshold level and can show evidence of adequate recordkeeping. Pre-reform law in Guatemala did not allow voluntary registration.

Zero-Rating and Exemptions

Two approaches are commonly used to lighten the burden of the VAT for specific sectors, activities, or commodities: zero-rating and exemptions. Under zero-rating there is no tax on the final sale, and taxes on all inputs are refunded. When the objective is to eliminate the tax on the consumption of a good, the right approach is zero-rating. Zero-Rating is commonly used in the VAT treatment of exports but not so commonly used to forgive tax on necessities (Ireland and the United Kingdom are two notable exceptions). Presumably, many countries feel that even necessities should bear some tax. A major disadvantage of zero-rating is that it imposes a substantial hit on the tax base, and if used in concert with exemptions, imposes substantial administrative costs.

Exemption from tax (which does not rebate the tax paid on inputs) is used when it is desired to decrease, but not entirely eliminate, the tax burden. This is frequently the case for food and medicines. Exemption is also used when it is not administratively possible to tax the good or service, as in the case of financial transactions. Among the problems with the exemption approach is the arbitrariness of input allocations among exempt and non-exempt activities. For example, most developing countries exempt one kind or another of foodstuffs, usually on grounds that such exemption makes the tax less regressive. Unprocessed food and food sold by small traders are commonly excluded from tax, but other countries have gone further and identified certain categories of food for exemption. The decision rules about what is a necessary foodstuff can become arbitrary, and the administration of the tax can become complicated (Due 1988, Chapter 8; Bird 1991, pp. 503-504). Most analysts of the VAT agree that apart from those necessities that occupy a large share of the budgets of the poor, and certain goods produced in the hard-to-tax sector, there is not a good case for exemption under the VAT.

The pre-reform Guatemalan system did not have a long list of exempt and zero-rated goods, but there was clearly room for base broadening:

- Exports were zero-rated. "Traditional exports" were taxable.
- Sales to the central government were taxable, but sales to municipalities were not taxable.
- Sales to registered private schools were not subject to tax but sales to public schools were taxable.
- Sales to public hospitals were taxable, but the services they provide were not taxed.
- Medicaments were taxed only at the import and manufacturing levels. Manufacturers paid tax on inputs, but no tax was charged on subsequent sales and no credit could be claimed.
- A detailed list of zero-rated and exempt foods was provided by the tax authorities. Supermarkets and other stores were required to distinguish between taxable and nontaxable foods. In general, food sales were zero-rated only if the items were sold in un-sealed containers. Thus canned fruit and vegetables were taxable, as well as packaged frozen foods; food in plastic sacks and cardboard boxes were not taxed. Fish, meat, and seafood were taxed, packaged or not. Certain items were zero-rated even if packaged, e.g., infant food, milk, and bread.
- There was no exemption of farms, per se, but registered farms received input tax credit. Some farms, mostly coffee plantations, were large enough to be registered. Most farm inputs were not zero-rated; the exception was most seed. Livestock, livestock feed, and fertilizer were taxed when sold by registered firms. Producers of traditional export farm products were not required to register, even if they exceeded the threshold, as long as they did not sell any portion of their products domestically.
- Excise goods, cigarettes, beer, and soft drinks, were taxed at the factory level on the retail price as set, and thus included the excise in the taxable price. They were not taxed at subsequent points of sale (unless, for example, served in a restaurants). Wine and distilled spirits were taxed at the factory on the factory price and on subsequent sales.
- The first 150 kwh of electricity for each household were zero-rated. The remainder, and all industrial use, was taxed at the full VAT rate.

- Water service was zero-rated when delivered through pipes.

From this list of exclusions, the following were considered by the Project for inclusion in the base:

- All pre-reform zero-rated domestic sales, including basic foods, such as unprocessed fruits and vegetables, grains and flour, milk, butter, coffee, sugar, salt, and corn tortillas; seeds; fuels; books and magazines; school supplies and educational materials; piped water; and 150 kwh of electricity per month for households.
- Exempt sales by coffee and sugar cane merchants, land transportation services, construction, funeral services, and entertainment.

Input Tax Credits

One of the basic advantages of the VAT over other forms of sales tax is that it eliminates (or reduces) cascading by allowing credits for taxes paid on all inputs. To the extent credit is not allowed on all business inputs, some of this advantage is lost. In Guatemala, the line between purchases for which input tax credit was allowed and those for which it was not allowed was unclear and arbitrary in the pre-reform period (Birch and Due 1990). In general, registered firms did receive input tax credit against tax due on their sales. There were, however, various exceptions and some rather fine delineation lines:

- Goods directly consumed in production as materials, or consumables such as electricity and fuel, were creditable.
- Input tax credit on the purchase of industrial machinery and equipment could be taken only over a 5-year period. Input tax credit on rental machinery and equipment could be taken in one year.
- Input tax on durable items not used up in production but used for administrative or support purposes was not subject to credit, for example, typewriters, store refrigerators, cash registers, display counters, etc.
- Legal services to manufacturers were creditable. Purchase of electricity by manufacturers, wholesalers, and retailers were creditable. Telephone service provided in a factory was eligible for input tax credit, but service in the headquarters of the firm was not. Other firms received input tax credit for one phone line only; a lawyer could receive input tax credit for all telephone service.

These exceptions, and many others like them, created a price distortion, provided an incentive for evasion, and complicated administration of the tax. Arbitrary rules that denied credit for some inputs but not others gave away some of the fundamental advantages of the value-added tax.

Credits for Capital Purchases

The pre-reform system required that credits for tax paid on capital purchases be claimed over a 5-year period. This feature raised the relative price of capital inputs, complicated enforcement, encouraged tax evasion and avoidance, and introduced some cascading. The reason for this special treatment of capital goods was to protect revenues. However, it defeated one of the principal advantages of the VAT, i.e., not to discriminate against investment. Many other countries have faced this problem e.g., Brazil, Spain, but in recent years have begun to move more fully to VAT as a consumption tax.

Refunds

Under the VAT, a refund is due when a firm's input tax credit is greater than its tax due on sales. This occurs for those who sell zero-rated goods (exporters) but also may occur when a firm faces unfavorable economic conditions, makes an inordinately heavy capital investment, and sells at a lower VAT rate than it pays on purchases. Good VAT practice calls for prompt payment of refunds, so that a "hidden" business tax will not develop. Tait (1988, p. 287) notes that most European Common Market countries pay excess credits within one month.

In theory, Guatemalan VAT payers were entitled to a refund when tax credits exceeded liability. Eighty percent of the refund was paid upon verification of the claim submitted by the taxpayer, and the remaining 20 percent was paid after completion of a field audit. In fact, the review and audit process was cumbersome, and a large backlog of unpaid refunds had accumulated by 1990. This was a source of considerable dissatisfaction on the part of businessmen.

The practice in Guatemala was not markedly different from that in many developing countries. The payment of refunds was slowed to avoid the revenue cost, and, in fact, delayed refunds could be viewed as a form of additional tax. Approximately one-half of all firms that filed returns, also filed for refunds.[5] Another reason refunds were not paid promptly was that the audit capacity of the government was not strong, and there was a fear that many of the applicants were not legitimately due refunds.

There is some evidence that this claim was well founded. Many of the returns already processed remained unclaimed. Apparently, some taxpayers preferred to forgo the refund rather than subject themselves to a field audit (Birch and Due 1990, p. 29).

The reform of the Guatemala system had to address this issue, notwithstanding the potential revenue loss. Taxpayers, especially investors, needed confidence that the government would stand by the promises in the tax law. At the same time the government would have to strengthen its audit capabilities.

Proposals for Reform

The Project proposed that these problems with the value-added tax could be addressed with a comprehensive program of structural and administrative reforms. The basic approach in the reform involved a broadening of the tax base to increase revenue and simplify administration, and a restructuring of the tax to allow for proper tax credit on inputs.

Tax Rate

The Project recommended an increase in the VAT rate to 10 percent. This would have left Guatemala well within the range of rates imposed by other countries. The revenue effects would have been considerable. If no changes had been made in the tax base or in the administration, adoption of a 10 percent rate would have increased revenues about 43 percent above the expected yield of the pre-reform system in fiscal year 1992.

The government decided to hold the nominal rate at 7 percent, and to look for increased revenues by broadening the VAT base. There are many reasons why the government was not willing to accept this proposal. The jump from 7 to 10 percent gave the appearance of being an increase in taxes (more so than base expansion would have); there was fear that an increased rate of VAT (and no increase in the rate of income tax) would be perceived as a regressive reform; and there was still a public memory of an unpopular reform in 1983 that increased the VAT rate to 10 percent, only to have it rolled back three months later. Finally, though the Guatemalan rate was low by world standards, there were a prevalence of low rates in Central America, e.g., Costa Rica (8 percent), Panama (5 percent), Honduras (7 percent), and Nicaragua (10 percent).

The proposed rate increase was never a serious contender for major reform. Though it would have imposed less of an administrative burden than would any of the other possibilities, it was not desirable for more reasons than those previously noted. Most important, it would have magnified all of the other structural flaws in the system by taxing at the higher rate. The cascading problem would have been worse, the negative impacts of the hidden tax and refund policy would have increased, and the bias against capital investment would have been greater.

Input Credits

The Project recommended that immediate credit be allowed for taxes paid on capital inputs and for the purchase of all inputs. This proposal was accepted by the government and was enacted. Clearly this proposal implied a revenue cost, but the estimated revenue loss was smaller than might have been expected. As may be seen in Table 7.2, it was estimated that the capital purchases credit would cost about Q100 million in 1994, an amount equivalent to about 6.5 percent of estimated total collections in that year if there were no other changes in the law. But the arguments for this reform went well beyond revenue considerations. They removed the bias against capital investment that was inherent in the prevailing practice, and they moved the tax closer to a true value-added levy by allowing credit on all inputs in the production process and therefore reduced price distortions.

Threshold Level

The Project recommended that the VAT exemption level be increased from Q12,000 to Q60,000, and that firms with gross sales below Q60,000 not be required to register. The government did increase the exemption level to Q60,000, but all firms were required to register for VAT. The revenue loss due to this change is nominal, especially when the administrative savings are considered.

Zero-Ratings

The Project recommended eliminating all zero-ratings, except for exports. The government accepted this proposal. It entailed extending the zero-rating status to traditional exports, and eliminating this status for petroleum products, most food and medicines, utilities, and printed products. The revenue consequences are described in Table 7.2. The extension of zero-rating to traditional exports was estimated to cost an amount equivalent to about 5 percent of the amount of revenues that would have been expected in 1993 in the absence of reform. By contrast, the elimination of zero-rating on those categories of domestic consump-

TABLE 7.2: Value-Added Tax Reforms: Revenue Implications

	Revenue Effect (FY94)	
	Amount (Millions of Quetzales)	Percentage of Baseline Revenue
Eliminate Zero-Rating of Basic Foods and Seeds	Q564	37.2%
Eliminate Zero-Rating of Petroleum Products	247	15.9
Eliminate Zero-Rating of School Supplies and Publishing	80	5.2
Eliminate Zero-Rating of Electricity	10	0.6
Eliminate the Exemptions of Medicines	13	0.8
Eliminate All Other Exempt Sales	47	3.0
Allow Full Credit for Tax on Capital Goods	-100	-6.5
Allow Firms to Claim Credit for Tax on All Business Purchases	-266	-17.1
Extend Zero-Rating to Traditional Exports	-85	-5.5
Include Stamp Taxes under the VAT	191	12.3
Refund Tax to Exempt Institutions	-109	-7.0
Total	Q592	38.2%

Source: Estimates from KMPG model, based on data from Ministry of Finance, Government of Guatemala, as reported to *Consultoria Para La Administracion Fiscal*, Policy Economics Group, KPMG Peat Marwick, and Policy Research Program, Georgia State University, 1991-1993.

tion previously noted should have increased revenues significantly. The estimates for 1994 were that these measures would increase revenues about Q900 million or nearly the combination of 60 percent over the expected yield under the present system. This was the most important revenue measure in the proposed reform.

Exemptions

The Project recommended elimination of all exemptions except for those mandated in the Guatemalan constitution and those for financial transactions. In general, the new law follows this rule. Exemptions are allowed for foodstuff purchases under Q100 (in markets), and for financial transactions carried out by banks. Real estate purchases are exempt if they meet two tests: the area must be less than 100 square meters, and the value must be less than Q100,000. All else—food, medicine, transportation services—are taxed. (For certain items exempted by the constitution, the government had been collecting the tax and then refunding the exempt entitlements. However, the court has now ruled this to be unconstitutional.) The estimated revenue loss from this change is equivalent to about 4 percent of 1994 collections.

Refunds

The Project recommended that all refunds be paid fully and without deferral. The practice of not paying net input tax credits promptly, or not paying at all, was disastrous in terms of taxpayer morale, and in terms of the incentive it promoted avoidance and evasion. Unfortunately, it was not possible to estimate the amount of revenue involved, but there were at least Q45 million of claims outstanding, and some private-sector sources believe the amount was significantly higher. This proposal was adopted.

Stamp Duties

Merge stamp duties with the value-added tax. The Project recommended that the government de-emphasize the existing stamp duty and move several categories of transactions into the value-added tax. To some extent, the new law incorporated this recommendation. Items transferred from stamp duty to value-added tax are estimated to increase value-added tax revenue by 13 percent. This is not necessarily an incremental amount, since there is an offsetting reduction in stamp duty revenues. With the switch to the value-added tax, however, the elasticity of the revenue yield from these items may be greater, and therefore the revenue yield may be greater in the long run. It may also be the case that the value-added tax will lead to a more effective enforcement of these taxes than did the stamp duty.

The Impact of the Reform

The VAT reform was projected to increase revenues by about 38 percent over what the pre-reform system would have yielded in 1993 and 1994 (see Table 7.2). This is a significant increase in revenues, and is accomplished primarily by base broadening through the elimination of a number of zero-rated categories. By contrast, an increase in the tax rate to 10 percent on the base of the previous system, by our estimate, would have yielded a 43 percent revenue increase. These estimates assumed no change in the rate of compliance and no behavioral responses by consumers or producers. The reformed system is expected to increase the effective VAT rate from 2.8 to 4.1 percent.

The revenue elasticity, however, is estimated to be lower in 1994 under the reform program than under the existing system (Table 7.3). These results come from the inclusion of slower growing items (necessity consumption) in the tax base, and from the exclusion of some faster-

TABLE 7.3: Value-Added Tax Reform: Estimated Impacts

1. Revenue Impact:

	(Fiscal Years, Q million)		
	1992	1993	1994
Baseline Projection	Q1,188	Q1,358	Q1,550
Tax Modernization Program	1,405	1,891	2,142
Difference	217	533	592
Tax Liability GDP Elasticity			
Baseline Projection	NA	1.02	1.04
Tax Modernization Program	NA	.87	.95

2. Tax Burden Impact (1992):

	Baseline		Tax Modernization Program	
Household Income Class	Number of Households (thousands)	Effective Tax Rate	Effective Tax Rate	Difference in Effective Tax Burden
Under Q2,465	180.9	0.8%	1.5%	0.8%
Q2,465 - 3,750	182.2	0.9	1.6	0.7
Q3,750 - 5,250	181.5	1.2	2.1	0.9
Q5,250 - 7,250	182.4	1.5	2.6	1.1
Q7,250 - 9,450	181.3	1.5	2.5	1.0
Q9,450 - 12,700	182.9	2.0	3.3	1.3
Q12,700 - 17,600	182.4	2.4	3.9	1.5
Q17,600 - 25,550	181.3	2.7	4.2	1.6
Q25,550 - 43,250	181.5	3.1	4.9	1.7
Q43,250 and Over	183.4	3.1	4.3	1.2
Q43,250 - 74,450	93.3	3.5	5.2	1.8
Q74,450 - 230,000	71.6	3.3	4.7	1.4
Over Q230,000	18.5	2.7	3.5	0.8
Total	1,819.7	2.8	4.1	1.3

Source: Ministry of Finance, Government of Guatemala, as reported to *Consultoria Para La Administracion Fiscal*, Policy Economics Group, KPMG Peat Marwick, and Policy Research Program, Georgia State University, 1991-1993.

growing components of total consumption (e.g., purchase of capital goods, certain business purchases, traditional exports).[6] The results in Table 7.3 suggest that by the mid-1990s, a 10 percent increase in GDP under the old system would have led to a 10.4 percent increase in VAT revenues, but under the new system would lead only to a 9.5 percent increase.

There are important caveats to the finding that the reform would lead to a lower revenue-income elasticity. In the past, the large number of zero-rated and exempt categories of consumption left substantial room for tax evasion. With the reductions in the number of exempt and zero-rated categories, evasion could become more difficult, and the reduction in the elasticity may not be so great. In this case, more transactions will be captured in the tax net, and the elasticity as well as the tax yield will be higher than is estimated here.

The vertical equity of the VAT is not markedly affected by the reform. Galper and Ramos (1992) have estimated the distribution of burdens of the VAT before and after the reform, using a simulation analysis. Their results are presented in the bottom panel of Table 7.3, and the far right column shows the change in the effective tax rate. As may be seen from these results, with the exception of the highest decile of income earners, there is no significant change in the degree to which the VAT burdens are distributed across income classes. For both the baseline and the reform case, burdens rise for all of the first nine income deciles, and the increases are progressive, i.e., the increase in the effective tax rate rises with income level.

The level of VAT burden has been ratcheted up for all taxpayers. For example, those in the bottom three deciles will see tax increases equivalent to less than 1 percent of income, while those in the middle-income brackets will see increases of 1.5 percent of income, or more. The top decile of income earners, and especially the top 1 percent, are out of line with this pattern. In fact, the top decile of income earners is estimated to realize an effective tax rate increase of 1.2 percent of income, which is less than the national average increase of 1.3 percent. The inclusion of more consumption goods in the VAT base is the principal reason for the smaller increase in the tax burden on these families. As a result, it can be said that the top end regressivity of the VAT has been increased by the reform.

Other Indirect Taxes

In fiscal year 1990, all other indirect taxes in the system (chiefly excises and stamp duties) accounted for about 20 percent of revenues.[7] The Project recommended significant changes in these levies.

Stamp Taxes

When the value-added tax was adopted in Guatemala, it replaced a stamp tax on the sale of commodities, but the remaining stamp taxes—mostly on commercial and legal documents—remained in effect when the transactions involved were not subject to the VAT. This was an attempt to reach a number of transactions that could not easily be included under the VAT, particularly those arising from financial transactions. The tax rates were 3 percent on most documents, 1 percent on some financial transactions, and 5 percent on lottery tickets. Galper and Ramos (1992) estimated that the distribution of the burden of the stamp tax under the pre-reform system was progressive, a not unexpected result, because the demand for legal documents would be expected to be income-elastic.

The stamp tax was an anomaly—a carryover from colonial times that has come to be regarded as obsolete in most countries. It has nuisance features, as any tax requiring application of stamps has, and it may have adverse effects on issuance of financial securities and official registration of transactions. The most objectionable effect, however, was the encouragement given to sellers to avoid issuing receipts, a practice that interferes with the enforcement of both the VAT and the income tax. In Guatemala, as in other countries, it was a difficult tax to enforce effectively. It must be admitted, however, that a self-enforcement feature comes from the taxpayers' desire to hold legally binding documents and the provision in the law that makes documents without the proper stamp taxes not legally binding.

The main arguments for eliminating the stamp duty have to do with its nuisance features and how it compromises the administrative efficiency of the VAT. However, its total elimination would have imposed a measurable revenue loss. The idea of replacing the stamp duty is not new. In 1983, the government replaced the stamp duty with a VAT, but eventually brought back the stamp in order to protect revenues. To make up for the potential revenue loss in 1992, a value-added tax rate increase of about 1.1 percent would have been required. Until such time as many financial transactions (which now constitute the bulk of collections) could be reached with the VAT, the Project recommend that stamp taxes be retained on these items. The Project also recommended introducing flexibility in the form of payment of the tax, thus moving away from the issuance of stamps. The government decided to integrate a portion of the stamp tax in the VAT base (see the previous discussion) and adopted more flexible forms for the payment of the tax, including stamping machines and cash payments through banks.

Excises

Excises, which apply to both domestic production and imports, were limited to the traditional commodities: tobacco products, alcoholic beverages, soft drinks, and petroleum products. Administration was in the hands of the Fiscalization Department of the Ministry, except for petroleum products, which were administered by the Bank of Guatemala.

In the case of cigarettes, beer, wine, and alcohol, the VAT was also levied at the manufacturing and import levels on the pre-established retail price.

There is much to recommend an excise tax system to accompany a value-added tax, especially in a developing country. Cnossen (1991) lists the advantages, in order of importance, as certainty and administrative feasibility, efficiency in the allocation of resources, and distributional equity. Most important, excises are an efficient way to raise revenue, especially when the tax administration system is thought to be weak.

Government officials, however, were extremely sensitive to the issue of whether any increase would bring Guatemala out of line with other countries in the region. Comparison of excise tax burdens among countries is difficult. In general, however, the burdens on beer and cigarettes were more or less comparable to those in other Latin American countries, perhaps a bit on the high side. But some countries—Ecuador, for example—had ad valorem rates more than twice as high as those in Guatemala. The tax on wine was low in comparison with the Caribbean commonwealth countries but above average for Latin American countries. The tax on distilled spirits was low in comparison to most countries.

The tax on gasoline was quite low compared to most countries and had fallen sharply between the mid-eighties and the middle of 1990. Because of price subsidies, the price of gasoline was low relative to other countries, and diesel fuel users were heavily subsidized over this period. A particularly strong case could have been made for increasing the tax on motor fuels because of the considerable price subsidy given to petroleum products. Even with a severalfold increase in the gasoline tax, however, the charge to operators of private cars would have remained substantially below the road-use cost they imposed and below international prices.

The Project recommended an increase in the tax on motor fuels of 50 percent. Purely on revenue grounds, the Project recommended an increase in the excise tax on alcohol and tobacco by 50 percent. This would not bring Guatemala much out of line with other countries (at least in the case of alcohol and tobacco), and would yield substantial revenues. The government finally decided to substitute the ad valorem tax on petroleum with a specific tax of 2 quetzals per gallon. The government also eliminated the zero-rating status of petroleum products under the VAT and all petroleum subsidies. The more significant revenue and equity impacts of the change in the tax on petroleum products were through the value-added tax. The tax rates on alcohol and tobacco were not increased.

Galper and Ramos (1992) estimated that the distribution of the burden of excise taxes was progressive under the pre-reform system, primarily because of the influence of the tax on petroleum products. The effect of the reform program was to leave the progressivity of the excise tax system intact but to significantly reduce the overall effective rate because of the shift of some excises to the VAT base.

Transport Taxes

Many countries have recognized the rapid increase in motor vehicle population and have moved to bring taxes in the transport sector into line with the growing costs of road construction and maintenance.[8] Although the motor vehicle population has grown rapidly in Guatemala, revenue growth from road user charges and taxes has been slow (Smith 1990). The income elasticity for these revenues as a whole has been low, although it has varied among different sources. The main sources of transport tax revenues were fuel taxes, taxes on the purchase and importation of motor vehicles, and annual registration fees. Customs duties on cars ranged from 30 to 40 percent of the cost including freight value. Those on trucks and buses were 5 percent and 15 percent, respectively. The 7 percent VAT was collected on cars but not on commercial vehicles. Although import duty revenues on motor vehicles rose rapidly from 1986 through 1988, this was in part due to the devaluation of the quetzal. VAT revenues from automobiles also increased between 1986 to 1988, but not nearly as rapidly as did customs duties.

Specific rather than ad valorem annual registration fees were levied on cars from 1955 to 1988. Annual registration fees have been based on the estimated value of cars since 1988. Although this revenue source has been income inelastic in the past, even with the growth in vehicle population, it should be much more elastic in the future. Fees on trucks and buses continued on a specific basis after 1988.

In light of the government's revenue needs, and with both efficiency and equity effects in mind, two other changes in the taxation of the transport sector were proposed by the Project. In neither case was there a significant revenue consequence.

The first proposal was to increase the import duty rate on trucks and buses from 5 to 15 percent. In the case of trucks, it was recommended that the full VAT rate be applied. This is another means by which large trucks can be charged to cover their road-damage costs. Because adequate disaggregation data are not available, an exact estimate of the revenue cost of this provision could not be made. The government adopted this measure.

The second proposal was to double the annual registration fees for motor vehicles. It was recommended that much of the increase come from additional fees on diesel trucks and buses to compensate for low diesel fuel taxes required because of off-road uses of diesel fuel. Although weight-distance taxes would have been desirable, administrative problems dictated that annual registration charges be based on vehicle weight. However, low bus registration fees may be warranted to the extent that subsidization is desired to keep bus fares low, in order to achieve income distribution objectives and to keep public transport from being overpriced relative to private transport. It was not possible to make a detailed estimate of the revenue effects of this proposed change. Based on collections in 1988, we estimated that a doubling of these fees (with full compliance) would produce approximately Q25 million in additional revenue in 1992.[9] The government did not adopt this measure.

Custom Duties

Taxes on international trade, import tariffs and export duties, have always been an important part of economic policy and government revenues in Guatemala.[10] Taxes on international trade represented, on average, one-third of all tax collections for the past three decades, but their importance had decreased. In 1991, custom duties represented 18.6 percent of revenue collections. Galper and Ramos (1992) estimated that the burden of custom duties was distributed progressively over most of the income distribution but with some top-end regressivity.

The protective tariff policies of the past were replaced with policies to make Guatemala's economy more open and competitive. The government has liberalized the foreign exchange market, eliminated taxes on exports, and lowered and simplified the customs tariff. Guatemala joined GATT in 1991, and—in an agreement with other members of the Central American Common Market (CACM) in 1991—set the goal of a unified tariff structure with a maximum rate of 20 percent and a minimum rate of 5 percent. Tariff rates were reformed to a range of 5 to 30 percent in 1992.

To further liberalize the international sector and ensure harmony with the tax reform proposals, the Project recommended to the government the reductions of the maximum tariff rates from 30 to 20 percent, the elimination of a 3 percent surcharge on all imports, the reform of Part III of the tariff (which among other things exempted the importation of oil products) and the elimination of many other exemptions.[11] The losses implied by the reduction in tariff rates are partially offset by the elimination of the exemptions, but the entire package would cost the government an estimated 114 million quetzals in 1993 and 130 million in 1994. The government implemented many of these proposed reforms during 1993, but the Project was unable to estimate the revenue impacts.

Property Taxation

The Guatemalan property tax is a self-assessed levy on the nationwide real property holdings of taxpayers, administered by the Ministry of Finance.[12] Rates are progressive, ranging from 0 percent on values of less than Q2001 to 0.9 percent on values above Q70,000. Tax liabilities are concentrated among relatively few taxpayers, with 3.8 percent of taxpayers responsible for about two-thirds of tax revenues. Galper and Ramos (1992) estimated the distribution of property tax burdens were progressive over most of the income range but regressive at the top end of the income scale. This is a surprising result given the expected skewed distribution of land ownership. Total revenues have increased at a rapid 23.9 percent annual rate over the past decade, but most of the growth occurred during the two years when structural changes were made.

Problems with the System

Several shortcomings in the existing structure were identified. First, the tax was likely to be horizontally inequitable because (1) taxable values are determined by self-assessment, (2) values had not been updated for several years, and (3) only about one-third to one-half of potential taxpayers were on the tax rolls.[13] Second, property tax administration appeared inadequate. Problems included a data processing system that was very poorly organized and unable to perform the most basic functions, poor handling of taxpayer accounts, and redundant systems. Also, no effort was being made to expand the cadastre or to independently appraise property.

Property tax revenues were low compared with other developing countries. Tanzi (1987) lists tax liabilities for a sample of 78 developing countries. The median country raised 0.36 percent of GDP in property and wealth taxes, compared with 0.13 percent in Guatemala. Further, there was a tendency for more prosperous developing countries, such as Guatemala, to raise a larger share of GDP from the property tax. Countries with greater than $850 per capita in GDP (in real 1981 dollars) raised more than 0.5 percent of GDP in wealth and property taxes, a level well above that in Guatemala. The share of taxes collected from the property tax was more in line with other countries, reflecting the overall low level of taxes in Guatemala. The median country raised 2.09 percent of total tax revenues with property and wealth taxes, compared with 1.98 percent in Guatemala. Again, developing countries with higher levels of income raise a greater share from the property tax, with the norm being above 3.0 percent.

Proposed Reform

The government proposed to enact a tax on land to replace the existing property tax. A Land Tax decree was drafted, with the following proposed features:

- The base of the tax would be square meters of land. Buildings would not be in the tax base, so it approached a pure site value tax.
- The proposed tax rate would be set up in zones, i.e., x quetzals per square meter in zone 1, y quetzals in zone 2, etc. A schedule prepared by the MOF was included in the draft decree. It was proposed that the rates be increased every three years by Guatemalan congress, based on proposals by the local governments. There would be no traditional valuation.
- Liability would be with those who were clear owners or had long-term leases for the use of land.
- The division of revenues was a contested issue. The government's initial proposal was that the revenues would be divided into four segments: that which goes to the local government where the collection was made (L); that which goes directly to the central government (C); that which goes to cover the cost of administration (A); and, that which goes into an equalization fund to be distributed to poorer local governments (E). The initial division proposed by the government was 40 percent (L), including the cost of their administration; 20 percent (E); 30 percent (C); and 10 percent (A) for those local governments who could not handle their own administration. The equalization pool would be distributed among the 332 municipalities on a basis of services available, the population level, and the resource base of the community, i.e., the demand for services and the capacity to finance those services. The Ministry of Finance would determine the distribution.
- There would be the usual exemptions, i.e., government buildings, religious buildings, charitable institutions, etc. In addition, plots less than 100 square meters would be exempt in urban areas, and less than 2 hectares would be exempt in rural areas.
- Every local government would keep its own land registry and its own record of accounts. Collection would be by the local governments or by the banks.
- The Ministry estimated that an additional 100 million quetzals in revenues could be obtained from the new property tax. This was

about 2 percent of projected revenues and well less than 0.5 percent of GDP.

There are many arguments to support this proposal. First, the present system was not working. Second, this simple system can work more effectively than a tax on land and improvements because no parcel-by-parcel valuation would be required. Third, the land tax might be justified on grounds of stimulating housing investment and renovation and of lessening the administrative burden.[14] A land tax also should be progressive in its distribution of tax burdens, since the ownership of land is concentrated in the higher income brackets (Bahl 1979).

There are criticisms of this approach, and shortcomings of the government proposal. One might argue that it is a very big administrative job for relatively little revenue, and that a larger yield is required to justify this change. Second, there is no tough penalty for nonpayment. The proposal is for a relatively small penalty plus interest, but this is not likely to discourage evaders in times of high inflation. Third, there is a substantial exemption list, and this will weigh heavily in Guatemala City, where government property and much other tax exempt property is located but where these buildings and their workers make use of municipal services. Most of the rest of the problems are administrative: Who will be liable for payment in the absence of clear title? Who will complete the land registry and at what cost? Who oversees the effectiveness of the local government administration?

There are other general criticisms of the proposal. A land tax does not reach tangible property wealth, and therefore does not tax luxury consumption as much as it should. Also, this proposed system would not establish values for individual plots of land but would assume homogeneity of land within an area. This may be an erroneous assumption and lead to horizontal inequities.

On balance, however, Guatemala could benefit from a land tax, not because it will be a major revenue producer, but because it will provide a tax on wealth and provide some balance to the system. The rates proposed, however, would not appear to generate enough revenue to justify the increased administrative cost implied.

Notes

1. The evaluation of the pre-reform Guatemalan system presented in this chapter draws heavily on Due (1989) and Birch and Due (1990).

2. Most analysts prefer a simplified rate structure, i.e., a single basic rate and perhaps a luxury rate, on grounds of simplifying administration (Tait 1988, pp.

33-34; Cnossen 1982; Harberger 1990, p. 30; and Due 1988, pp. 144-46). The IMF also sees a single-rate VAT as a preferred option (Tanzi 1991, p. 165). Other analysts believe that a single-rate VAT is not compatible with all of the goals the government has set for the tax and prefer a number of rates under a joint VAT and excise regime (Ahmed and Stern 1991 pp. 215-18).

3. But some other countries do use more than one criteria. Mexico, for example, uses three rules: (1) income must not exceed more than thirty-two times the minimum wage; (2) there may be no more than three employees; and (3) business space must be no more than 50 square meters (Tait 1991, p. 14).

4. Due (1988, chapter 8) identifies six separate or joint criteria for determining the threshold for sales tax liability: sales volume, capital investment or profit, mechanization in production, number of employees, exemption by type of industry, and exclusion by administrative action.

5. This may not be an unusual proportion for a developing country. Tait (1988, p. 285) reports, for example, that one third of all filers claim a VAT refund in Panama.

6. These are plausible explanations, but even so, the revenue-income elasticity of the VAT in Guatemala appears quite low by international standards. Most studies have found the revenue income elasticity of sales taxes in developing countries to be well in excess of unity (Due 1988, pp. 206-207).

7. This section draws heavily on Birch and Due (1990); Due (1989); Greaney, Mizrahi and Covert (1992a); Stacey (1991) and Smith (1990).

8. This section draws heavily from Smith (1990).

9. For more detail, see Smith (1990).

10. This section draws heavily from Wisecarver (1992).

11. For detail, see Bahl, Martinez-Vazquez, and Wallace (1994). There is an important caveat to these revenue estimates. Microsimulation models with no adjustment for behavioral effects, as are used here, may not be suitable for making estimates of the revenue impact of adjustments in trade policy. As noted by Blejer and Cheasty (1990, page 72), "the initial impact of trade liberalization on the volume of trade tax collections cannot be predicted in any simple way." They argue that it is necessary to sort out the impact of five principal determinants of the fiscal impact: (1) the price and income elasticities of the demand for imports; (2) the elasticity of substitution between imports; (3) the market structure of import trade; (4) announcement effects; and (5) exchange rate adjustments.

12. This section draws on Fox (1991) and Greytak (1989).

13. Pineda (1992, pp. 122-123) reports that in the four largest urban areas, about 2 million assessments were expected in 1991, but only 1.2 million were received.

14. For an analysis of the performance of the land value base in a developing country, see Holland and Follain (1990).

8

Impact of the Reform Program
and Next Steps

The Guatemalan tax reform was directed mostly at a structural reform, and in large measure it achieved this goal. The reform has three priority objectives: to remove distortions in relative prices that affect economic choices; to improve the fairness of the system by removing arbitrary preferential treatments; and to simplify the tax system, thereby making administration easier. The general strategy was to broaden the tax base and lower the tax rate. The following improvements have been introduced:

- The taxation of interest, which lessens the incentive for debt finance and reduces the possibility of negative real tax rates that characterized the system.
- The removal of all tax incentives (except those for export promotion) in order to put more businesses on an equal footing.
- The provision of refunds under the VAT to eliminate a hidden tax and a disincentive to comply fully with the tax.
- The allowance of full and immediate credit for capital purchases and the allowance of credit for all inputs to remove the existence of cascading, an important distortion in the value-added tax.
- The extension of zero-rating to traditional exports to put invest- ment in all types of export activities on the same footing and enhance the competitive world position of Guatemalan traditional exports.
- The elimination of the average-marginal rates under the income taxes to remove a significant incentive to understate income and to engage in some form of transfer pricing in order to avoid a substantial tax penalty from changing tax brackets.

The horizontal dimension of equity also concerns the equal treatment of families in "similar" circumstances. A tax system is fair if it offers equal treatment, and this stimulates public confidence and compliance. The Guatemalan reform did improve the fairness of the tax system. In this respect, there are three important revisions to the individual income tax: (1) By bringing interest income into the tax net, the reform lessens the differential treatment of families who receive their income from wages and those who receive their income from interest. (2) Among wage earners, the taxation of bonus income provides equity by removing preferential treatment. (3) The use of a single general deduction will be easier to police, and therefore will reduce tax evasion (which by itself is an important source of horizontal inequity).

Simplification of the tax structure was also achieved, though with modernization of the economy there is no real escape from increased complication in some tax areas (Bahl and Martinez-Vazquez 1992). Still, the reformed system is in many ways less complicated. The three most significant changes in this regard are (1) replacing the present complicated system of deductions with a single standard deduction, (2) eliminating zero-rating for several consumption and production activities, and (3) eliminating exemptions for others. The pre-reform system was almost impossible to monitor effectively because there were so many separate deductions and so many separate treatments of consumption items. The broader-based VAT and income tax system will allow tax inspectors to shift their efforts from classification-type activities to the more revenue-productive audit and collection functions.

The reform program did not have increased revenue mobilization as its primary goal. The main purpose of the analytic policy work was always to identify a more efficient tax structure and then leave it to the political process to decide on the right level of tax rates. The Project estimated the revenue impacts of each reform option, always with the objective of hitting the revenue-neutral level of GNP—the tax share of GDP was about 8 percent in 1989. As the government revised its targets for overall revenue mobilization, the Project estimated the impact of alternative rate levels and alternative base expansions. But the primary emphasis of the Project was on structure and not on raising revenue.

The revenue impact of the full reform program is summarized in Table 8.1. The estimates were that the reform program would increase the tax share of GDP from its 1991 level of 7.5 percent to a level of 8.1 percent in 1994. Had the reform not been enacted, the Project estimated that the tax share of GDP would have reached no more than 7.7 percent by 1994. Taxes were projected to be 5 percent (Q266 million) higher in 1994 than they would have been in the absence of the reform. In fact, the true revenue impact of the reform could be much larger. Projections for

TABLE 8.1: Comprehensive Reform: Estimated Impact

	(Fiscal Years, Q million)		
	1992	*1993*	*1994*
1. Revenue Impact:			
Baseline Projection	Q3,939	Q4,521	Q5,322
Tax Modernization Program	4,279	5,186	5,588
Difference	340	430	266
2. Revenue Impact (Percent of GDP):			
Baseline Projection	7.5%	7.5%	7.7%
Tax Modernization Program	8.1	8.2	8.1
3. Tax Liability - GDP Elasticity:			
Baseline Projection	NA	1.03	1.27
Tax Modernization Program	NA	1.10	0.93

4. Tax Burden Impact (1992):

Household Income Class	*Effective Tax Rate*		
	Present System	*Tax Moderniza- tion Project*	*Difference*
Under Q2,465	7.2%	7.7%	0.5%
Q2,465 - 3,750	7.1	7.6	0.5
Q3,750 - 5,250	7.5	8.2	0.7
Q5,250 - 7,250	7.8	8.8	1.0
Q7,250 - 9,450	6.8	7.8	1.0
Q9,450 - 12,700	8.6	9.8	1.2
Q12,700 - 17,600	8.9	10.3	1.4
Q17,600 - 25,550	9.4	11.0	1.6
Q25,550 - 43,250	9.7	11.5	1.8
Q43,250 and Over	11.2	11.9	0.7
Q43,250 - 74,450	9.6	11.6	2.0
Q74,450 - 230,000	11.1	12.2	1.1
Over Q230,000	12.1	11.8	-0.3
Total	10.2%	11.2%	1.0%

Source: Ministry of Finance, Government of Guatemala, as reported to *Consultoria Para La Administracion Fiscal*, Policy Economics Group, KPMG Peat Marwick, and Policy Research Program, Georgia State University, 1991-1993.

the pre-reform system assumed no change in the compliance rate, no discretionary adjustments in the tax structure, and no behavioral responses to the new system.

One consequence of the reform is a shift in revenue reliance away from the income tax and toward indirect taxes. The Project estimated that by 1994, the proportion of revenues generated by income taxes would have been about 28 percent in the absence of reform, but would be about

19 percent because of the reform (see Table 8.2). The Project estimated that the VAT would be more than 38 percent of total taxes, in comparison with 29 percent if no reform had been undertaken.

Ordinarily, a shift from income taxation to VAT would reduce the overall elasticity of the system. In fact, this happened in the case of the Guatemala reform, as the income elasticity dropped to 0.93 from the 1.27 that (theoretically) would have existed in the absence of the reform. However, the high elasticity of the pre-reform system would not in all probability have been realized because of a declining compliance rate.

Vertical equity was not harmed by the tax reform. Guatemala is known to have one of the more unequal income distributions in the world. It also has one of the lowest levels of taxation. The government's objective in this tax reform program was more in the direction of investment enhancement and job creation than in establishing a large direct fiscal transfer of income to the poor. The Project estimated that the net effect of the tax system changes were consistent with this objective.

The project estimated that the tax-modernization program would increase the average tax burden from 10.2 percent to an estimated 11.2 percent of income, based on 1992 data. The distribution of the tax burdens remains progressive through the first nine income deciles (higher income families have experienced a greater increase in the effective rate), as was the case under the pre-reform system. For the highest 10 percent of income earners, however, the increase in the effective rate is only about equal to the national average, and as a result, the top-end progressivity of the system is less than that of the pre-reform system.[1]

TABLE 8.2: Tax Structure: Pre-reform and Tax Modernization Program Estimates for 1994 (Percentage of Total Revenue)

	Pre-reform	Tax Moderni-zation Program
Income Taxes	28.1%	19.3%
Individuals	(7.7)	(3.6)
Businesses	(20.4)	(15.8)
VAT	29.1	38.5
Customs Duties	22.5	21.5
Excise Taxes	14.7	15.9
All Others	5.6	5.3
TOTAL	100.0%	100.0%

Source: Ministry of Finance, Government of Guatemala, as reported to *Consultoria Para La Administracion Fiscal*, Policy Economics Group, KPMG Peat Marwick, and Policy Research Program, Georgia State University, 1991-1993.

In sum, what can be said about the accomplishments of the Guatemalan tax reform is that it achieved most of the objectives that were set for it. It created a more level playing field for business decisions by broadening the tax base, it simplified the system and set the stage for an improved administration, and it did not markedly diminish the existing progressivity of the system. The revenue consequences of the reform reflect some choices that the government made in the process of this restructuring: the tax rates were kept low, and therefore the revenue share of GDP was kept low, and there was a shift in emphasis away from income taxation to indirect taxation.

The Unfinished Agenda: Next Steps in Tax Reform

The Tax Modernization Program of 1992 significantly improved the Guatemalan tax structure. The new system is simpler, easier to administer and comply with, more investor friendly, and more fair. Most important, the reformed system removes many of the distortions to relative prices that previously had affected economic choices. Moreover, an administrative infrastructure has been put in place to support the government's efforts to increase the rate of compliance. The system is now much broader-based, and it has retained relatively low rates. If rate increases are to be considered in the future, they may be taken on a more comprehensive base.

The government may wish to turn to the task of increased revenue mobilization, a policy objective that long has been urged by the World Bank and IMF. A target level of revenues equivalent to 12 to 15 percent of GDP was widely discussed in Guatemala and was identified by some officials as being needed for the support of an essential level of public expenditures. Moreover, international norms for tax effort would suggest a target ratio of taxes to GNP in the 12 to 15 percent range. The tax modernization plan, however, will not allow the government to reach a revenue target of 12 to 15 percent of GDP by 1994. As may be seen from Table 8.1, the tax modernization program adopted by the government was estimated to increase Guatemala's tax ratio to about 8 percent in 1994.

It is also important to note that the revenue share of GDP will not increase automatically as the economy grows, i.e., the revenue-income elasticity of the system under the modernization plan is less than unity. In other words, the tax share of GDP will decrease over time unless there are revenue enhancing discretionary rate and base changes, administrative improvements, or supply-side effects that will increase the amount of economic activity coming into the tax net. The shift in reliance away from the income tax, the broader VAT base, and the adoption of less progressive tax rate schedules are reasons for this reduced elasticity. (The other side of this issue is that a less elastic system is also less sensitive to fluctuations in economic activity, hence more stable in its yield.) If the efficiency of the tax administration falters, or if the taxpayer compliance rate deteriorates, the revenue growth could be even slower.

In fact, the tax ratio did rise from 7.37 percent of GDP in 1991 to 8.39 percent in 1992 but fell off to 7.85 percent in 1993. The IDB (1994, page 94) attributes this falloff in taxes to a reduction in tariff rates and increased evasion. The Project estimates anticipated this decline but for a different reason—the lower elasticity of the reformed tax system.

The policy routes open for increasing revenues by as much as 4 percent of GDP almost certainly must include rate increases. Moreover, there is more to do on the structural and administrative reforms. The following possibilities are not inconsistent with the objectives of the tax modernization program and might be considered in the next round of reforms.

Increase the Value-Added Tax Rate

An increase from 7 to 10 percent on the reformed base would raise an amount equivalent to about 1.3 percent of GDP. There is much to recommend this possible reform. Perhaps, most important, it would move the government significantly closer to its revenue target. There is probably little hope of reaching the goal of a 4 percent increase in the tax rates without a significant VAT increase. There are other advantages that recommend this action. Because the revenue would be raised on the new broader base of value-added, it would not lend additional distortions to the economy. Finally, a 10 percent rate would not be out of line with worldwide VAT rates.

An increase in the VAT rate is likely to be a controversial option in Guatemala and, in fact, was rejected as a component of the 1992 reform. Certainly it would add to the concern about the top-end regressivity of the system, i.e., that with each reform the tax system becomes more regressive. In particular it would be argued to favor the top decile of income earners, where Guatemala's wealth holdings are thought to be concentrated. Another critique is that this change would not add to the income elasticity of the tax system. This rate increase by itself would merely increase the revenue reliance on VAT and therefore would not enhance the automatic growth in revenues. Nevertheless, an increase in the VAT rate remains an important possibility for the government, and has significant advantages.

Broaden the Individual Income Tax Base

A first step would be to eliminate the VAT credit and the exemption of the Christmas bonus. These changes have much to recommend them. The VAT credit is no more than an additional reduction in tax liability, and because it cannot be administered, it has no effect on the collection efficiency of the value-added tax. It results in the exclusion of a significant number of potential taxpayers from the rolls, reduces the progressivity of the tax system, and reduces the revenue-income elasticity of the tax system.

The Christmas bonus provides a welcome deduction to some Guatemalan taxpayers. Though it seems that a tax-free Christmas bonus could do any harm, the fact is that this exemption causes a revenue loss and is unfair in that it does not treat all income taxpayers the same. Moreover, the revenue loss must be made up, probably with an increase in the rate of another tax, and so the unfairness is exacerbated. The elimination of the VAT credit and the Christmas bonus tax preferences was expected to increase tax revenues by an estimated Q167 million in 1994, an amount equivalent to less than 0.3 percent of GDP.

Do Not Index the Individual Income Tax

The Project recommended that the individual income tax not be indexed for inflation. A better strategy for Guatemala is to allow the population to grow into the present income tax structure. One reason for the low yield of the individual income tax in Guatemala is that the threshold for taxation is so high. Only the top decile of income earners pay the tax. By allowing the real value of the deductions to erode, the coverage of the tax could be expanded to a greater proportion of the population. This strategy would also increase the income elasticity of the individual income tax. This is one case where inflation can work to improve the overall tax structure.

Adopt a Global Income Tax

The individual income tax should offer the same treatment to all sources of income: wages, interest, dividends, rents, and capital gains. Though interest is not taxed, it is given a preferential rate. In the future, the tax rate on interest income should be increased to the top marginal rate applied to wage and salary income. The same should be done for capital gains. These measures would increase revenues (by an estimated Q70 million in 1994, about 0.1 percent of GDP in the case of interest income alone), and it would increase the revenue-income elasticity of the tax system. It also would make the tax system more progressive, because interest income tends to accrue to those in the top brackets, and would lessen some of the top-end regressivity of the reformed system. Such a reform would also make the system more horizontally equitable, because wages, interest income, and dividend income would be treated the same.

The argument against the full taxation of interest income is capital flight—higher taxes on interest income will simply encourage capital to seek an offshore home to increase the after-tax return. The evidence for capital flight potential would not seem to defeat the advantages of full taxation of interest.

Increase the Compliance Rate

A poor tax administration can defeat the goals of even the best legal tax structure. Guatemala has serious problems with the administration of its tax system, and as a result, some of the desirable effects of increasing the compliance rate may be lost. Improved enforcement is a necessary condition for the success of this structural reform.

The compliance rate for the VAT was weak in the pre-reform period. In estimating the revenue yield for the reform period, we have assumed only that it will not grow worse. As reported in Table 3.9, the gap under the VAT between taxable purchases and taxable sales was equivalent to more than 56 percent of taxable purchases. This suggests significant room for revenue increase under the present system, even without discretionary changes.

A national income accounts approach was undertaken to estimate the unreported income under the individual and company income taxes. The results, presented for 1986 in Table 3.10, show that the gap is significant. The Project estimated reported income from the income tax return data at 8.3 billion quetzals. Analysis of the national income accounts data suggest that it should have been in the range of 16 billion quetzals, i.e., reported income was about half of what it should have been. Clearly, there is significant room to expand the base of the individual and business income taxes through administrative measures.

Impose a Land Tax

There is much to recommend the imposition of a land tax. It would bring some form of tax on wealthholding—a part of the tax base that is not now reached by the Guatemalan tax system. It would add some progressivity to the tax system, since landholdings are concentrated in the hands of higher income Guatemalans. It would also provide a revenue source for local government finances, thereby relieving some of the pressure on the central government budget.

There are two major problems with the land tax as an option for reform. One is that it is not likely to address long-term revenue problems, because its yield will almost certainly be small. According to initial government proposals, a land tax would raise an amount no more than 0.3 percent of GDP. The second problem is that at any but nominal rates, a land tax is likely to be politically difficult to sell to voters.

Increase the Income Tax Rates

There is room to increase the rates of the company and individual income taxes and not get out of line with rates in competitor countries. Increased rates would have the advantage of increasing the yield and elasticity of the overall tax structure but would have the disadvantage of possibly discouraging investment.

Notes

1.   It is important to note that these calculations probably overstate the progressivity of the system (pre-reform and post-reform) to the extent they do not fully account for the earnings of the higher-income self-employed, who are not in the tax net.

APPENDIX A
Individual Income Tax Microsimulation Models

The technical estimates of the effects of the individual income tax reform were calculated using a microsimulation model. Microsimulation models are tools of revenue estimation that are based on individual or microlevel data. These models enable analysts to calculate the effects of changes in the tax law on tax liabilities, tax burdens, and tax payments, using individual level observations of individuals (or firms).

Individual income tax microsimulation models include three parts: a microlevel data base (typically information from tax returns for individuals for a base year, supplemented with data from a national consumer expenditure or household survey), a tax calculator (a computer program that calculates the tax paid under alternative tax structures), and an output program that categorizes taxes paid by income group, tax burdens, "winners and losers," and the overall change in tax liability.[1]

The data used in the model usually come from a sample of taxpayers, as was done for Guatemala, and contain all relevant information from the tax returns. Additional data may be imputed to each tax observation. For example, it may be useful to know the consumption pattern of the taxpayers. In Guatemala, such imputations were made by merging the tax return data with data from the National Income and Expenditure Survey. This type of merge provides more detailed information about taxpayers, and it also adds observations for individuals with no tax liability. These data are taken from some base year, usually the most recent tax filing year. The data can then be extrapolated or "aged" using macroeconomic aggregates. In Guatemala, the aggregates were developed from data provided by the Bank of Guatemala.

The tax calculator is a straightforward computer program that calculates the actual tax liability for each individual observation in the data set based on current law. By changing the program to reflect changes in the tax law, the analyst can "simulate" new tax liabilities for any number of proposals.

The microsimulation models used in this project were developed by KPMG Peat Marwick. These are described in Bachrach and Covert (1992), Bachrach and Mizrahi (1993), Greaney, Mizrahi and Covert (1992a, 1992b), Newland and Beckwith (1992a, 1992b), and Vasquez, Madrigal and Greaney (1989).

---

[1]For more technical information regarding these models see U.S. Treasury (1990), Edwards and Wallace (1995), and Bahl, Hawkins, Moore, and Sjoquist (1993).

References

Advisory Commission on Intergovernmental Relations. 1991. *State Revenue Capacity and Tax Effort*. Washington D.C.: ACIR.

Ahmad, Ehtisham, and Nicholas Stern. 1991. *The Theory and Practice of Tax Reform in Developing Countries*. Cambridge, Great Britain: Cambridge University Press.

Alm James, Roy Bahl, and Matthew Murray. 1991a. "An Evaluation of the Structure of the Jamaican Individual Income Tax." In *The Jamaican Tax Reform*, ed. Roy Bahl, 87-152. Boston: Lincoln Institute of Land Policy.

_____. 1991b. "A Program for Reform." In *The Jamaican Tax Reform*, ed. Roy Bahl, 153-80. Boston: Lincoln Institute of Land Policy.

Auerbach, Alan. 1984. "Taxes, Firm Financial Policy and the Cost of Capital: An Empirical Analysis," *Journal of Public Economics* 23 (February/March): 27-57.

Austin, Oakley. 1989. *Tax Administration*. Technical Memorandum No. 3. Guatemala Fiscal Administration Project. Atlanta: Georgia State University, College of Business Administration, Policy Research Center; Washington, D.C.: KPMG Peat Marwick Policy Economics Group.

Bachrach, Carlos, and Ranel Covert. 1992. *The Computable General Equilibrium Model for Guatemala: User Manual*. Technical Memorandum No. 30. Guatemala Fiscal Administration Project. Atlanta: Georgia State University, College of Business Administration, Policy Research Center; Washington D.C.: KPMG Peat Marwick Policy Economics Group.

Bachrach, Carlos and Lorris Mizrahi. 1993. *The Computable General Equilibrium Model for Guatemala: Technical Manual*. Technical Memorandum No. 31. Guatemala Fiscal Administration Project. Atlanta: Georgia State University, College of Business Administration, Policy Research Center; Washington D.C.: KPMG Peat Marwick Policy Economics Group.

Bahl, Roy. 1971. "A Regression Approach to Tax Effort and Tax Ratio Analysis." *International Monetary Fund Staff Papers* 18, No. 3 (November): 570-612. Washington, D.C.: International Monetary Fund.

_____. 1972. "A Representative Tax System Approach to Measuring Tax Effort in Developing Countries." *International Monetary Fund Staff Papers.* Reprint (March): 87-124. Washington, D.C.: International Monetary Fund.

_____, ed. 1979. "The Practice of Urban Property Taxation in Less Developed Countries." In *The Taxation of Urban Property in Less Developed Countries: Proceedings of a Symposium at the Lincoln Institute, Cambridge, Mass: 1976,* by the Committee on Taxation, Resources and Economic Development (TRED). Madison, Wis.: University of Wisconsin Press.

_____. 1991a. *The Jamaican Tax Reform.* Boston: Lincoln Institute of Land Policy.

_____. 1991b. "The Economics and Politics of the Jamaican Tax Reform." In *The Jamaican Tax Reform,* ed. Roy Bahl, 1-60. Cambridge, Mass.: Lincoln Institute of Land Policy.

Bahl, Roy, Richard Hawkins, Robert E. Moore, and David L. Sjoquist. 1993. "Using Microsimulation Models for Revenue Forecasting in Developing Countries." *Public Budgeting and Financial Management* 5 No. 1: 159-86.

Bahl, Roy, and Jorge Martinez-Vazquez. 1992. "The Nexus of Tax Administration and Tax Policy in Jamaica and Guatemala." In *Improving Tax Administration in Developing Countries,* ed. Richard Bird and Milka Casanegra de Jantscher, 66-110. Washington, D.C.: International Monetary Fund.

Bahl, Roy, Jorge Martinez-Vazquez, Michael Jordan, and Sally Wallace. 1993. "Intercountry Comparisons of Fiscal Performance." Technical Note No. 7. Guatemala Fiscal Administration Project. Atlanta: Georgia State University, College of Business Administration, Policy Research Center; Washington, D.C.: KPMG Peat Marwick Policy Economics Group.

Bahl, Roy, Jorge Martinez-Vazquez, and Sally Wallace. 1994. "The Guatemalan Tax Reform: Final Policy." Technical Note No. 33. Guatemala Fiscal Administration Project. Atlanta: Georgia State University, College of Business Administration, Policy Research Center; Washington, D.C.: KPMG Peat Marwick Policy Economics Group.

Ballentine, Greg, and Charles McLure. 1980. "Taxation and Corporate Financial Policy." *Quarterly Journal of Economics* 94 (March): 350-72.

Barham, Vicky, Satya Poddar, and John Whalley. 1987. "The Tax Treatment of Insurance Under a Consumption Type, Destination Basis VAT." *National Tax Journal* 60 (June): 171.

Biderman, Kenneth, and John Tucillo. 1976. *Taxation and Regulation of the Savings and Loan Industry,* Lexington, Ky: Lexington Books.

Birch, Melissa. 1989. *Public Enterprise Sector.* Technical Memorandum No. 4.

Guatemala Fiscal Administration Project. Atlanta: Georgia State University, College of Business Administration, Policy Research Center; Washington, D.C.: KPMG Peat Marwick Policy Economics Group.

_____. 1991. *The Guatemalan Public Enterprise System: Selected Issues*. Technical Memorandum No. 21. Guatemala Fiscal Administration Project. Atlanta: Georgia State University, College of Business Administration, Policy Research Center; Washington, D.C.: KPMG Peat Marwick Policy Economics Group.

Birch, Melissa, and John Due. 1990. *Indirect Taxation in Guatemala*. Technical Memorandum No. 11. Guatemala Fiscal Administration Project. Atlanta: Georgia State University, College of Business Administration, Policy Research Center; Washington, D.C.: KPMG Peat Marwick Policy Economics Group.

Bird, Richard M. 1976. *Charging for Public Services*. Toronto: Canadian Tax Foundation.

_____. 1980. *Tax Incentives for Investment: The State of the Art*. Canadian Tax Paper No. 64. Toronto: Canadian Tax Foundation.

_____. 1982. "Taxation and Employment in Developing Countries." *Finanzarchiv* 40, No. 2: 211-39.

_____. 1989. "Taxation in Papua New Guinea: Backwards to the Future?" *World Development* 17: 1145-57.

_____. 1991. "Choosing a Rate Structure." In *The Jamaican Tax Reform*, ed. Roy Bahl, 503-504. Cambridge, Mass.: Lincoln Institute of Land Policy.

_____. 1992. *Tax Policy and Economic Development*. Baltimore: The Johns Hopkins University Press.

Bird, Richard M., and Milka Casanegrade. 1992. *Improving Tax Administration in Developing Countries*. Washington D.C.: International Monetary Fund.

Bird, Richard M., and Oliver Oldman. 1990. *Taxation in Developing Countries*. Baltimore: The Johns Hopkins University Press.

Blejer, Mario, and Adrienne Cheasty. 1990. "Fiscal Implications of Trade Liberalization." *Fiscal Policy in Open Developing Economies*, ed. Vito Tanzi. Washington, D.C.: International Monetary Fund.

Boadway, Robin W. 1988. "The Theory and Measurement of Effective Tax Rates." In *The Impact of Taxation on Business Activity*, ed. Jack Mintz and Douglas Purvis. Kingston: John Deutsch Institute.

Boadway, Robin W., Neil Bruce, and Jack Mintz. 1982. *Corporate Taxation in*

Canada: Toward an Efficient System. Canadian Tax Paper No. 66, ed. Wayne R. Thirsk and John Whalley. Toronto: Canadian Tax Foundation.

_____. 1987. *Taxes on Capital Income in Canada: Analysis and Policy.* Canadian Tax Paper No. 80. Toronto: Canadian Tax Foundation.

Boskin, Michael J. 1978. "Taxation, Saving, and the Rate of Interest." *Journal of Political Economy* 86 (April): 53-528.

Bovenberg, Alan. 1989. "Tax Policy and National Saving in the United States: A Survey." *National Tax Journal* 42 (June): 123-38

Bradford, David F., and Don Fullerton. 1981. "Pitfalls in the Construction and Use of Effective Tax Rates." In *Depreciation, Inflation and the Taxation of Income from Capital,* ed. Charles R. Hulten. Washington, D.C.: The Urban Institute.

Brannon, Gerald. 1990. *Preliminary Report on the Taxation of Financial Institutions in Guatemala.* Technical Memorandum No. 16. Guatemala Fiscal Administration Project. Atlanta: Georgia State University, College of Business Administration, Policy Research Center; Washington, D.C.: KPMG Peat Marwick Policy Economics Group.

Break, George. 1991. "The Jamaican Income Tax System: A Framework for Policy Formation." In *The Jamaican Tax Reform,* ed. Roy Bahl, 63-87. Cambridge, Mass.: Lincoln Institute of Land Policy.

Burgess, Robin, and Nicholas Stern. 1993. "Taxation and Development." *Journal of Economic Literature* 31 (June): 762-830.

Byrne, Peter D. 1994. "The Business Assets Tax in Latin America—No Credit Where It's Due." *Tax Notes International* (August 15): 533-38.

Chelliah, Raja J. 1971. "Trends in Taxation in Developing Countries." *International Monetary Fund Staff Papers* 18, No. 3 (November): 570-612. Washington, D.C.: International Monetary Fund.

Chelliah, Raja J., Hessel Baas and Margaret Kelly. 1975. "Tax Ratios and Tax Effort in Developing Countries, 1969-1971." *International Monetary Fund Staff Papers* 22, No. 1 (March): 187-205.

Clotfelter, Charles. 1983. "Tax Evasion and Tax Rates: An Analysis of Individual Returns." *Review of Economics and Statistics* 65 (August): 363-73.

Cnossen, Sijbren. 1982. "What Rate Structure for a Value-Added Tax." In *National Tax Journal* 35 (June): 205-14.

_____. 1991. "The Extended Excise Tax System." In *The Jamaican Tax Reform*, ed. Roy Bahl, 537-56. Boston: Lincoln Institute of Land Policy.

Coburn, F. Marion. 1990. "Returns Processing, Receipts Processing, Tax Roll and Vehicle Registration." Technical Note No. 5. Guatemala Fiscal Administration Project. Atlanta: Georgia State University, College of Business Administration, Policy Research Center; Washington, D.C.: KPMG Peat Marwick Policy Economics Group.

de la Cuadra, Sergio. 1990. "A Note on the Monetary Problem in the Context of a Possible Program with the IMF." Technical Note No. 6. Guatemala Fiscal Administration Project. Atlanta: Georgia State University, College of Business Administration, Policy Research Center; Washington, D.C.: KPMG Peat Marwick Policy Economics Group.

Due, John. 1988. *Indirect Taxation in Developing Economies*, rev. ed. Ed. Vernon Ruttan and T. Paul Schultz. Baltimore: The Johns Hopkins University Press.

_____. 1989. *Internal Indirect Taxation*. Technical Memorandum No. 6. Guatemala Fiscal Administration Project. Washington, D.C.: KPMG Peat Marwick Policy Economics Group; Atlanta: Georgia State University, College of Business Administration, Policy Research Center.

Edwards, Barbara, and Sally Wallace. 1995. "State and Local Individual Income Taxes: Analysis and Options." In *Taxation and Economics Development in Ohio: A Blueprint for Tax Reform*, ed. Roy Bahl, 221-82. Columbus, Ohio: Battelle Press.

Estache, A. 1990. "Minimum Taxes Levied on Business Activities: A Brief Introduction to Design Issues and an Application to Brazil." Mimeograph. Washington D.C.: The World Bank.

Fox, William. 1991. *The Property Tax in Guatemala: Its Present Structure and Future Prospects*. Technical Memorandum No. 23. Guatemala Fiscal Administration Project. Atlanta: Georgia State University, College of Business Administration, Policy Research Center; Washington, D.C.: KPMG Peat Marwick Policy Economics Group.

_____. 1995. "Sales Tax: Current Condition and Policy Options." In *Taxation and Economics Development in Ohio: A Blueprint for Tax Reform*, ed. Roy Bahl, 221-82. Columbus, Ohio: Battelle Press.

Frenkel, Jacob A., Assaf Razim and Efraim Sadka. 1991. *International Taxation in an Integrated World*. Cambridge, Mass.: The MIT Press.

Gale, William, and John Karl Scholz. 1993. "IRAs and Household Savings." Mimeograph. Madison, Wis.: University of Wisconsin.

Galper, Harvey, Robert Lucke and Eric Toder. 1988. "A General Equilibrium Analysis of Tax Reform." In *Uneasy Compromise,* ed. H. Aaron. H. Galper and J. Pechman, 59-108. Washington D.C.: Brookings Institute.

Galper, Harvey, and Fernando Ramos. 1992. *The Incidence of Guatemalan Taxes.* Technical Memorandum No. 32. Guatemala Fiscal Administration Project. Atlanta: Georgia State University, College of Business Administration, Policy Research Center; Washington, D.C.: KPMG Peat Marwick Policy Economics Group.

Gandhi, Ved P., ed. 1987. *Supply Side Tax Policy: Its Relevance to Developing Countries,* Washington: International Monetary Fund.

Gersovitz, Mark. 1987. "Domestic Taxes and Foreign Private Investment." In *The Theory of Taxation for Developing Countries,* ed. David Newberry and Nicholas Stern. New York: Oxford University Press.

Gillis, Malcolm, ed. 1989. "Comprehensive Tax Reform: The Indonesian Experience, 1981-1988." In *Tax Reform in Developing Countries,* 79-114. Durham N.C.: Duke University Press.

Goode, Richard. 1984. *Government Finance in Developing Countries.* Washington D.C.: The Brookings Institution.

_____. 1993. "Tax Advice to Developing Countries: An Historical Survey." *World Development* Vol. 21, No. 1, pp. 37-53.

Greaney, Francis, Lorris Mizrahi, and Ranel Covert. 1992a. *The Indirect Tax Model for Guatemala: User's Manual.* Technical Memorandum No. 28. Guatemala Fiscal Administration Project. Atlanta: Georgia State University, College of Business Administration, Policy Research Center; Washington, D.C.: KPMG Peat Marwick Policy Economics Group.

_____. 1992b. *The Indirect Tax Model for Guatemala: Technical Manual.* Technical Memorandum No. 29. Guatemala Fiscal Administration Project. Atlanta: Georgia State University, College of Business Administration, Policy Research Center; Washington, D.C.: KPMG Peat Marwick Policy Economics Group.

Greytak, David. 1989. *Local Government Finance and Property Taxation.* Technical Memorandum No. 5. Guatemala Fiscal Administration Project. Atlanta: Georgia State University, College of Business Administration, Policy Research Center; Washington, D.C.: KPMG Peat Marwick Policy Economics Group.

Haig, Robert M. 1921. "The Concept of Income: Economic and Political Aspects."

In *The Federal Income Tax*, ed. Robert M. Haig. New York: Columbia University Press.

Hall, Robert, and Alvin Rabushka. 1995. *The Flat Tax*. Stanford CA: Hoover Institute Press.

Harberger, Arnold C. 1962. "The Incidence of the Corporation Income Tax." *Journal of Political Economy* 70: 215-40.

_____. 1981. "Tax Incentives." In *Fiscal Reform in Bolivia*, ed. R. Musgrave. Cambridge, Mass.: International Tax Program of the Harvard Law School.

_____. 1990. "Taxation in an Open Economy." In *Taxation in Developing Countries*, ed. R. Bird and O. Oldman, 4th Edition. Baltimore: Johns Hopkins University Press, 313-21.

Heller, Peter S., and Jack Diamond. 1990. "International Comparisons of Government Expenditure Revisited: The Developing Countries, 1975-1986." *Occasional Paper 69*. Washington, D.C.: International Monetary Fund.

Hines, James., and Glenn Hubbard. 1990. "Coming Home to America: Dividend Repatriations by U.S. Multinationals." In *Taxation in the Global Economy*, ed. A. Razin and J. Slemrod, 161-200. Chicago: University of Chicago Press.

Hoffman, Lorey, Satya Poddar, and John Whalley. 1987. "Taxation of Banking Services Under a Consumption Type Destination Value-Added Tax." *National Tax Journal*. 40 (December): 547-54.

Holland, Daniel, and James Follain. 1990. "The Property Tax in Jamaica." In *The Jamaican Tax Reform*, ed. Roy Bahl, 605-39. Boston, Mass.: Lincoln Institute of Land Policy.

Inter-American Development Bank. 1991. *Economic and Social Progress in Latin America: 1991 Report*. Washington, D.C.: Inter-American Development Bank. Distributed by The Johns Hopkins University Press.

_____. 1992. *Economic and Social Progress in Latin America: 1992 Report*. Washington, D.C.: Inter-American Development Bank. Distributed by the Johns Hopkins University Press.

International Monetary Fund. 1993. *World Economic Outlook*. Washington, D.C.: International Monetary Fund.

Johnson, Darwin, and Jaime Porras. 1989. *Analysis of the Budgeting System*. Technical Memorandum No. 9. Guatemala Fiscal Administration Project. Atlanta: Georgia State University, College of Business Administration, Policy

Research Center; Washington, D.C.: KPMG Peat Marwick Policy Economics Group.

King, Mervyn, and Don Fullerton. 1984. *The Taxation of Income from Capital.* Chicago: University of Chicago Press.

Lane, Malcolm. 1991. *Computerization of Fiscal Administration in Guatemala.* Technical Memorandum No. 15. Guatemala Fiscal Administration Project. Atlanta: Georgia State University, College of Business Administration, Policy Research Center; Washington, D.C.: KPMG Peat Marwick Policy Economics Group.

Leechor, Chad and Jack Mintz. 1990. *On the Taxation of Multinational Corporate Investment When the Deferred Method Is Used by the Capital Exporting Country.* Working Paper 9013, Canada: University of Toronto, Department of Economics.

Lotz, Joergen, and Elliot Morss. 1967. "Measuring Tax Effort in Developing Countries." *International Monetary Fund Staff Papers* 14, No. 3 (November): 478-99.

Martinez-Vazquez, Jorge. 1989. *Income and Payroll Taxes.* Technical Memorandum No. 7. Guatemala Fiscal Administration Project. Atlanta: Georgia State University, College of Business Administration, Policy Research Center; Washington, D.C.: KPMG Peat Marwick Policy Economics Group.

_____. 1991. "The Taxation of Financial Institutions in Jamaica." In *The Jamaican Tax Reform,* ed. Roy Bahl, 339-70. Boston, Mass.: Lincoln Institute of Land Policy.

McLure, Charles. 1989. *Taxation of Business, Commercial Policy, and Industrial Policy.* Technical Memorandum No. 2. Guatemala Fiscal Administration Project. Atlanta: Georgia State University, College of Business Administration, Policy Research Center; Washington, D.C.: KPMG Peat Marwick Policy Economics Group.

McLure, Charles, John Mutti, Victor Thuronyi, and George Zodrow. 1989. *The Taxation of Income from Business and Capital in Colombia.* Colombia, South America: Dirrecion General de Impuestos Nacionales.

McLure, Charles, and Pardo R. Santiago. 1992. "Improving the Administration of the Colombian Income Tax." In *Improving Tax Administration in Developing Countries,* ed. Richard Bird and Milka Casanegra de Jantscher, 124-44. Washington, D.C.: International Monetary Fund.

McOmber, Dale. 1991. *Improving the Budgeting Process.* Technical Memorandum

No. 19. Guatemala Fiscal Administration Project. Washington, D.C.: KPMG Peat Marwick Policy Economics Group.

Meade, J. E. 1978. *The Structure and Reform of Direct Taxation.* London: Allen and Unwin.

Mieszkowski, Peter. 1969. "Tax Incidence Theory: The Effects of Taxes on the Distribution of Income." *Journal of Economic Theory* 7: 1103-24.

Mintz, Jack. 1988. *Tax Holidays and Investment.* Washington, D.C.: The World Bank, Public Economics Division, CECEM.

_____. 1991. *Proposals for the Restructuring of the Corporate Income In Guatemala.* Technical Memorandum No. 12. Guatemala Fiscal Administration Project. Washington, D.C.: KPMG Peat Marwick Policy Economics Group.

Musgrave, Richard and Peggy Musgrave. 1984. *Public Finance in Theory and Practice.* New York: McGraw-Hill.

Mutti, John. 1991. *The Taxation of Foreign Source Enterprises and Foreign Source Income.* Technical Memorandum No. 17. Guatemala Fiscal Administration Project. Atlanta: Georgia State University, College of Business Administration, Policy Research Center; Washington, D.C.: KPMG Peat Marwick Policy Economics Group.

Nester, Howard. 1992. *Training in Fiscal Policy Analysis and Fiscal Models.* Technical Memorandum No. 24. Guatemala Fiscal Administration Project. Atlanta: Georgia State University, College of Business Administration, Policy Research Center; Washington, D.C.: KPMG Peat Marwick Policy Economics Group.

Newberry, David, and Nicholas Stern. 1987. *The Theory of Taxation in Developing Countries.* London: Oxford University Press.

Newland, Ned, and Stewart Beckwith. 1992a. *The Guatemala Business Income Tax Model: User's Manual.* Technical Memorandum No. 25. Guatemala Fiscal Administration Project. Atlanta: Georgia State University, College of Business Administration, Policy Research Center; Washington, D.C.: KPMG Peat Marwick Policy Economics Group.

_____. 1992b. *The Guatemala Business Income Tax Model: Technical Manual.* Technical Memorandum No. 26. Guatemala Fiscal Administration Project. Atlanta: Georgia State University, College of Business Administration, Policy Research Center; Washington, D.C.: KPMG Peat Marwick Policy Economics Group.

Pineda, Jaime S. 1992. "Comment on The Nexus of Tax Administration and Tax

Policy in Jamaica and Guatemala." In *Improving Tax Administration in Developing Countries,* ed. Richard Bird and Milka Casanegra de Jantscher, 124-44. Washington, D.C.: International Monetary Fund.

Porras, Jaime. 1991a. *Guatemala Government Budgeting: A Survey of the Budget System and Practices.* Technical Memorandum No. 20. Guatemala Fiscal Administration Project. Atlanta: Georgia State University, College of Business Administration, Policy Research Center; Washington, D.C.: KPMG Peat Marwick Policy Economics Group.

Rajaram, Anand. *Inflation and the Company Tax Base.* 1989. Working Paper Series No. 278. Washington, D.C.: The World Bank.

Ramos, Fernanado, and Wayne Thirsk. 1991. *Tax Incentives in Guatemala.* Technical Memorandum No. 14. Guatemala Fiscal Administration Project. Atlanta: Georgia State University, College of Business Administration, Policy Research Center; Washington, D.C.: KPMG Peat Marwick Policy Economics Group.

Royal Commission on Taxation. 1966. *Report of the Royal Commission on Taxation.* 6 Volumes. Ottawa: Royal Commission on Taxation.

Shah, Anwar, and Joel Slemrod. 1990. *Tax Sensitivity of Foreign Direct Investment.* Working Paper Series No. 434. Washington D.C.: The World Bank.

Shah, Anwar, and John Whalley. 1990. *An Alternative View of Tax Incidence Analysis of Developing Countries.* Working Paper Series No. 462. Washington, D.C.: The World Bank.

Shah, S.M.S, and J.F.J Toye. 1978. "Fiscal Incentives for Firms in Some Developing Countries: Survey and Critique." In *Taxation and Economic Development,* ed. J.F.J. Toye. London: Frank Cass.

Simons, Henry C. 1938. *Personal Income Taxation.* Chicago: University of Chicago Press.

Smith, Roger. 1990. *Fiscal Treatment of the Transport Sector in Guatemala.* Technical Memorandum No. 17. Guatemala Fiscal Administration Project. Atlanta: Georgia State University, College of Business Administration, Policy Research Center; Washington, D.C.: KPMG Peat Marwick Policy Economics Group.

Stacey, Kenneth. 1989a. *Customs and Export Incentive Administration Reform.* Technical Memorandum No. 1. Guatemala Fiscal Administration Project. Atlanta: Georgia State University, College of Business Administration, Policy Research Center; Washington, D.C.: KPMG Peat Marwick Policy Economics Group.

_____. 1989b. "Supplement to Technical Memorandum No. 1: Customs and

Export Incentive Administration Reform." Technical Note No. 1. Guatemala Fiscal Administration Project. Atlanta: Georgia State University, College of Business Administration, Policy Research Center; Washington, D.C.: KPMG Peat Marwick Policy Economics Group.

_____. 1989c. "Program for Customs Training." Technical Note No. 2. Guatemala Fiscal Administration Project. Atlanta: Georgia State University, College of Business Administration, Policy Research Center; Washington, D.C.: KPMG Peat Marwick Policy Economics Group.

_____. 1989d. "The UNDP Project for the Computerization of the Guatemalan Customs." Technical Note No. 3. Guatemala Fiscal Administration Project. Atlanta: Georgia State University, College of Business Administration, Policy Research Center; Washington, D.C.: KPMG Peat Marwick Policy Economics Group.

_____. 1989e. "Synopsis of Customs and Export Fiscal Incentives Project for the United States Ambassador." Technical Note No. 4. Guatemala Fiscal Administration Project. Atlanta: Georgia State University, College of Business Administration, Policy Research Center; Washington, D.C.: KPMG Peat Marwick Policy Economics Group.

_____. 1991. *Excise Tax Administration—Guatemala Issues and Findings*. Technical Memorandum No. 22. Guatemala Fiscal Administration Project. Atlanta: Georgia State University, College of Business Administration, Policy Research Center; Washington, D.C.: KPMG Peat Marwick Policy Economics Group.

Tait, Alan. 1988. *Value-Added Tax: International Practice and Problems*. Washington, D.C.: International Monetary Fund.

_____. 1991. "VAT Policy Issues: Structure, Regressivity, Inflation, and Exports." In *Value-Added Tax: Administrative and Policy Issues*. Occasional Paper 88, 1-15. Washington, D.C.: International Monetary Fund.

Tait, Alan, Wilfred Gratz, and Barry Eichengreen. 1979. Taxation in Jamaica. Unpublished report prepared for International Monetary Fund, Fiscal Affairs Department.

Tanzi, Vito and Parthasarathi Shome. 1993. "A Primer on Tax Evasion." *IMF Staff Papers* 40, No. 4 (December): pp. 807-828.

Tanzi, Vito. 1987. "Quantitative Characteristics of the Tax Systems of Developing Countries." In *The Theory of Taxation for Developing Countries*, ed. David Newberry and Nicholas Stern. New York: Oxford University Press for the World Bank.

Tanzi, Vito, ed. 1991. "Tax System and Policy Objectives in Developing Countries:

General Principles and Diagnostic Tests." In *Public Finance in Developing Countries*, 157-74. Brookfield, Vt: Edward Elgar Publishing Company.

Thirsk, Wayne. 1985. "Jamaican Tax Incentives. Jamaican Tax Structure Examination Project." Staff Paper No. 18. Jamaica: Board of Revenue. A shortened version of this paper appears in *Taxation in Development Countries*, ed. R. Bird and O. Oldman. Baltimore and London: Johns Hopkins University Press, 1990.

Thuronyi, Victor. 1990. *Company and Individual Income Taxation: Structure and Administration*. Technical Memorandum No. 10. Guatemala Fiscal Administration Project. Atlanta: Georgia State University, College of Business Administration, Policy Research Center; Washington, D.C.: KPMG Peat Marwick Policy Economics Group.

Usher, Dan. 1977. "The Economics of Tax Incentives to Encourage Investment in Less Developed Countries." *Journal of Economic Development* 4: 119-48.

Vasquez, Thomas, Sergio Madrigal, and Francis Greaney. 1989. *Tax and Fiscal Analysis and Modeling Capabilities*. Technical Memorandum No. 8. Guatemala Fiscal Administration Project. Atlanta: Georgia State University, College of Business Administration, Policy Research Center; Washington, D.C.: KPMG Peat Marwick Policy Economics Group.

Venti, Steven F. and David Wise. 1987. "IRAs and Savings." In *The Effects of Taxation on Income Accumulation*, ed. Martin Feldstein, 7-48. Chicago: University of Chicago Press.

Wasylenko, Michael. 1991. "Tax Burden Before and After Tax Reform." In *The Jamaica Tax Reform*. R. Bahl, ed. Cambridge, Mass.: Lincoln Institute of Land Policy.

Wisecarver, Daniel. 1992. *Taxes on International Trade in Guatemala*. Technical Memorandum No. 27. Guatemala Fiscal Administration Project. Atlanta; Georgia State University, College of Business Administration, Policy Research Center; Washington, D.C.: KPMG Peat Marwick Policy Economics Group.

Zodrow, George. 1990. *Marginal Effective Tax Rates on Capital Income in Guatemala*. Technical Memorandum No. 13. Guatemala Fiscal Administration Project. Atlanta: Georgia State University, College of Business Administration, Policy Research Center; Washington, D.C.: KPMG Peat Marwick Policy Economics Group.

About the Book and Authors

Responding to a deepening economic crisis, serious structural problems with the tax system, a long and deep-seated opposition to even modest tax increases, and a weak tax administration, the Guatemalan government introduced a comprehensive tax reform program in 1992. In this concise volume, the authors review the data that supported the creation of the reform program and evaluate the first round of revenues and tax-burden effects.

Focusing their theoretical and empirical analysis on revenue yield impacts, on effects of relative prices and relative tax treatment of different types of companies, and on the distribution of tax burdens by income class, the authors factor in individual and company income taxes, value-added tax, taxes on international trade, and property tax. In each case, they describe the existing tax system and evaluate it against the traditional norms; in addition, they analyze alternative structural reforms within the Guatemalan context.

Comprehensive tax reforms in less developed countries are infrequent, and the Guatemalan experience provides a fascinating case study of how modern analytic techniques can be used by policymakers to formulate tax structure changes. The authors also draw contrasts with experiences in other countries and revisit many of the principles that have been laid down for guiding tax reforms in developing nations.

Roy Bahl is professor of economics and public administration and director of the Policy Research Center at Georgia State University. He has written and consulted extensively on the subjects of tax policy and intergovernmental fiscal relations in developing countries. **Jorge Martinez-Vazquez** is professor of economics and associate director of the Policy Research Center at Georgia State University. He has published numerous journal articles in public finance and has extensive experience in transition and developing economies. **Sally Wallace** is assistant professor of economics and senior associate at the Policy Research Center at Georgia State University. She specializes in the analysis of federal and state-local taxation and savings issues in the United States as well as in transition and developing countries.